ISLAM & EUROPE
Challenges and Opportunities

Lectures Forum A. & A. Leysen 2006-2007

ISLAM & EUROPE
Challenges and Opportunities

Ludo ABICHT
Nasr ABU ZAYD
Sadik AL-AZM
Tariq ALI
John BOWEN
Roger DILLEMANS
Mark EYSKENS
Marie-Claire FOBLETS
André LEYSEN
Tariq MODOOD
Ruud PETERS
Jean-Pierre RONDAS
Bassam TIBI

UPL in Context

© 2008 Leuven University Press / Presses Universitaires de Louvain / Universitaire Pers Leuven

All rights reserved. Except in those cases expressly determined by law, no part of this publication may be multiplied, saved in an automated datafile or made public in any way whatsoever without the express prior written consent of the publishers.

ISBN 978 90 5867 672 6
D / 2008 / 1869 / 11
NUR: 741 / 717

Cover design: Jurgen Leemans
Typesetting: Friedemann Vervoort (Friedemann BVBA)

Table of Contents

Foreword – André Leysen   7

Introduction – Marie-Claire Foblets   9

Multiple Adaptations: Islam in Three Worlds – John Bowen   17
    * Questions & answers

The Poldermujahidin: The Radicalization   47
of Young Dutch Muslims – Ruud Peters

Islam and Europe in the Age of Intercivilizational Conflict.   63
Diversity and the Challenges – Bassam Tibi
    * Questions and answers

Muslim Integration and Secularism – Tariq Modood   85
    * Questions & answers

Islam, Muslims and the West: Religion and Secularism.   113
From Polarization to Negotiation – Nasr Abu Zayd

Science and Religion, an Uneasy Relationship in the History   127
of Judeo-Christian-Muslim Heritage – Sadik al-Azm
    * Introduction by Jean-Pierre Rondas: Islam's Satanic
      Tragedy as Described in Sadik al-Azm's Exegesis
    * Responses by Mark Eyskens and Roger Dillemans

Why are we so Obsessed by Islam? – Tariq Ali   159
    * Introduction by Ludo Abicht
    * Questions & answers

List of Contributors   187

Foreword

Welcome to this Forum, established by the Catholic University of Leuven together with the Leysen family. The two founders have opted for the socially relevant theme of intercultural relations, and this year in particular the relations between the western and the Islamic worlds. The presence of so many participants confirms that we are dealing with a very current topic. Professor Foblets will chair the proceedings, which means we can be assured of a valuable experience and innovative inspiration.

In 1428, Leuven university offered the future cardinal and papal legate Nicholas of Cusa a chair in canon law. In 1437 Cusa was sent by the pope to Constantinople in order to try to reconcile the eastern and western churches. His mission met with success. Unfortunately, that reconciliation was short-lived. On his way back to Italy, Cusa was overcome by the realisation of the coincidence of all apparent opposites. This he referred to as the *Coincidentia Oppositorum*. His insight, that over and above all contradictions there is something that unites, is more relevant than ever.

Each generation has its own distinctive task.
- My generation wanted to protect Europe from war and to unify it.
- The present generation must further develop and reinforce the existing attainments.
- The coming generation faces the enormous challenge of preventing the threatening polarisation between the worldview of the West and that of Islam.

Didn't Professor Emilio Platti say years ago already: "If the West does not engage in dialogue with moderate Islam, the whole world will become one great Northern Ireland."

Like Cusa, we must look for the *Coincidentia Oppositorum*, that which binds together beyond all contradiction. May his spirit be among us and his position be our guiding light.

André Leysen,
2 October 2006

Introduction to
The Anne & André Leysen Forum
on 'Intercultural relations'

The Anne & André Leysen Forum on *Intercultural relations* was founded at the Catholic University of Leuven in 2006 within the context of the programme of external Chairs. The activities of the Forum began in that same year.

The Forum is an initiative of Mr and Mrs Anne and André Leysen and their children, who as donors made it possible for a series of activities to be organised under the aegis of the K.U.Leuven around the theme of *Intercultural relations*.

The basic idea that inspired the establishment of a Forum on 'Intercultural relations' is the observation that our society is becoming ever more diverse. With the multiplication of the number of cultural groups and communities, and their increasing visibility in society, there is a growing need to know who these new communities are. What are their expectations with regard to their future here, not only in Flanders/Belgium, but also within Europe? How can we build a society with these new groups on a peaceful basis, and moreover in a way that is not regarded as a threat to the attainments of the welfare state and of democracy? It is noteworthy that in spite of increasing mediatisation and globalisation, for the most part little is known even today about the cultural background of the many new groups who have settled in Belgium since the post-war migrations.

The Anne & André Leysen Forum on *Intercultural relations* creates an opportunity to listen to a series of eminent experts speak on the broad theme of intercultural relations, and to engage in discussion with them.

For the first year of operation, the theme chosen was that of 'Islam in the contemporary world and in Europe'. Seven scholars came from abroad to give a lecture organised by the Forum. Each of them enjoys an indisputable international reputation in his field of expertise, and takes an active role in the public debate on the position of Islam in the world yesterday, today and tomorrow.

The speakers were asked to devote particular attention to the following topics: the relationship(s) between religion and the State; human rights and fundamental freedoms; specific problems relating to the context of migration; (ir)reconcilability with modernity; pluralism and freedom of expression; the conditions for cordial relations among the various religions in Europe and among the various orientations within Islam itself. The papers, along with a selection from the question and answer session with the audience, are published in this volume.

The first series of lectures took place within a limited circle. Around a hundred participants had pre-registered for the series. With this volume, we would like to make the lecture series more widely known.

The speakers differ quite significantly from each other in their views and in their analyses of the factors that make the relationships between Islam and Europe difficult today. But there is one conviction that unites them all, namely, that dialogue is essential if we wish to take a constructive approach to the challenge of the growing diversity in society. This conviction likewise underlies the initiative of the A. & A. Leysen Forum. The papers are printed in the order in which the speakers appeared.

The first paper is by **John Richard Bowen** (*Multiple Adaptations: Islam in Three Worlds*). He is an anthropologist and scholar of Islam at Washington University in St. Louis. In the 1980s and 90s he published extensively on Islam in Indonesia. For several years now he has been interested as well in Islam in France, and in the question of the spread of Islamic doctrine in western societies. He has researched, among other topics, the impact of the attacks of 11 September 2001 on the development of Islam throughout the world. In 2007 he published an anthropological analysis of the debate on the ban on wearing the headscarf in France (*Why the French Don't Like Headscarves. Islam, the State, and Public Space*, Princeton U.P.), which adopts an original perspective on the struggle to preserve 'secularity'. In his contribution to this volume, he reports on his experience in three different social contexts (the U.S., Indonesia and France) and shows how Muslim communities in each of these countries take a different approach to other groups within their society.

Ruud Peters (*The Poldermujahidin: the Radicalization of Young Dutch Muslims*) was the second speaker in this series. He is a special lecturer in Islamic law at the University of Amsterdam. He has many years of experience in the field of Islamic and Middle Eastern studies. In recent years he has also repeatedly provided expert advice to policymakers in a variety of dossiers. For instance, in 2001 he spent some time in Nigeria as an expert with the European Union. His task was to carry out a study of the reislamisation of criminal law in Northern Nigeria. More specifically, the question of the degree to which the reintroduction of Islamic criminal law in the region ran counter to the obligations to protect international human rights. Since 2001 he has also been serving regularly in the Netherlands as an expert witness, more particularly in trials involving radical Islamic groups. One such assignment led to the drafting of the expert report written, at the request of the Dutch prosecutor, for the investigation into the murder of the Dutch filmmaker Theo van Gogh. In his paper for this volume, Ruud Peters sums up the principal findings contained in that report. The radicalization of Muslim youth in the Netherlands is, according to Peters, not so much a matter of religion or faith, but of socio-economic disadvantage. That is all too easily forgotten.

Bassam Tibi (*Islam and Europe in the Age of Intercivilizational Conflict. Diversity and the Challenges*) is professor of International Relations at the University of Göttingen. He is considered one of the founders of 'Islamology', a social-scientifically oriented study of Islam. He was co-founder of the Arab organisation for human rights and is one of the delegates to the first Muslim-Jewish-Christian 'trialogue'. His publications include: *Europa ohne Identität? Die Krise der multikulturellen Gesellschaft* [Europe without identity? The crisis of the multicultural society], Bertelsmann, 1998. In his contribution to this volume he warns Europe of the consequences of its inability to engage in an open dialogue with Islam. Europe, according to Bassam Tibi, is engaged in an internal struggle: on the one hand, it is becoming ever more Eurocentric (neo-absolutism), and on the other hand it no longer knows what it stands for (cultural relativism). In such a context, there is no room for the kind of openness that would give Muslims a real chance to participate fully. The consequence is that Europe is thrown back upon itself, and this leads to the formation of radicalising enclaves, with all the risks which that implies. Based on the example of what Bassam Tibi was able to observe in Africa, he holds out the dream that over time, a more regional, European version of Islam will develop here, a sort of 'Euro-Islam' that should in no way be regarded as a threat, since it will have been shaped by Muslims who feel at home in Europe and identify with this continent. The real danger, according to Bassam Tibi, lies in an Islam that feels itself to be isolated in Europe, and is not recognised.

Tariq Modood (*Muslim Integration and Secularism*) is a British political philosopher of Pakistani origin. His is currently teaching at the University of Bristol. He is considered one of the most important theorists of multiculturalism in the United Kingdom today. His work has in recent years focused mainly on Muslims, a minority that he has helped gain a prominent place in the public debate about the future of British society. Tariq Modood's approach is an original one: one that he calls 'eclectic'. In his analysis he draws on theories from political philosophy which he seeks to connect with the daily experiences of British Muslims. In his work he tries to close the gap between theory and practice. The identity of Muslims is, according to Tariq Modood, shaped first of all by their religion. That is true also for British Muslims. In addition, racism has also played a role in the development of what Tariq Modood sees as a 'new ethnic assertiveness'. On the basis of his reflections on racism and religion, he makes a number of pragmatic recommendations for what he sees as a more consistent policy. His approach in any case makes for a new, critical view of British society. His work enjoys wide recognition beyond the United Kingdom as well. In his contribution to this volume, he draws inspiration from the following books he has published: *Multicultural Politics: Racism, Ethnicity and Muslims in Britain*, University of Minnesota Press and University of Edinburgh Press, 2005; T. Modood, A. Triandafyllidou and R. Zapata-Barrero (eds), *Multiculturalism, Muslims and Citizenship: A European Approach*, Routledge, 2006; *Multiculturalism: A Civic Idea,* Cambridge, Polity, 2007.

The fourth paper in this collection is by **Nasr Abu Zayd** (*Islam, Muslims and the West: Religion and Secularism. From Polarization to Negotiation*). Nasr Abu Zayd was for many years professor of Arabic studies at the University of Cairo, and is currently professor of Islamic studies at the Rijksuniversiteit Leiden in the Netherlands. He also holds the Ibn Rushd chair in humanism and Islam at the University of Utrecht. In the Arab-Islamic world he is considered one of the most important thinkers and renewers of his field, a position that has brought him into lively conflict with more conservative thinkers in Egypt and ultimately impelled him to move to the Netherlands, where he has since been granted refugee status. He is the author of, among other works, *Vernieuwing in het islamitisch denken* [Renewal in Islamic thought], Bulaaq, 1996; *Rethinking the Qu'rân: Towards a Humanistic Hermeneutic*, University of Humanistics, Utrecht, 2004. In his work, he seeks to develop a theology that enables Muslims to reconcile their own tradition(s) with the values and norms of the modern world, such as: freedom, equality, human rights and democracy. In his contribution to this volume he attributes to the West a large part of the responsibility for radicalising Islam in the Middle East and in countries such as Pakistan, India and Iran. Nasr Abu Zayd takes a strong position against what he calls the reactionary conceptions of the Islamists. But in this paper his purpose is not to attack the essence of Islamist views – he has done that elsewhere – but to point out the historical role which the Western

Introduction to The Anne & André Leysen Forum on 'Intercultural relations'

powers and intellectuals played, and still play, through their continued condescension towards Islam and by failing (not wanting) to understand the Islamic world or, what is worse, by wishing to dominate it to this day. The outcome is confrontation.

Sadik al-Azm *(Science and Religion, an Uneasy Relationship in the History of Judeo-Christian-Muslim Heritage)* holds a PhD from Yale and is emeritus professor of European philosophy at Damascus. Sadik al-Azm is a leading thinker with a broad international following. He was able to maintain a highly independent position in the debate of the second half of the twentieth century about relations between Arab social and political thought and Europe. Thus, from the 1960s he adopted a strongly critical stance with regard to the nationalistic-populist thought of the Arab world. To this day he remains critical of the contemporary social, political and religious debates within the Arab world. His paper reads as a testimony. During that period (1968) Sadik al-Azm was harshly punished when, as a professor at the American University in Beirut, he took a critical stance towards the interference of religion in scientific discussions. His book entitled *Critique of Religious Thought* was, despite strict censorship, a bestseller. His commitment to free, critical scientific research that does not allow itself to be dominated by religious concerns or interference has remained unchanged to this day. In his contribution to this volume he demonstrates that the struggle between science and religion has existed at all times, and is thus not unique to Islam. He also points to the risks of a political use of religious criteria, the goal of which is to clip the wings of scientific activity. In the past, that has always meant the end of a period of flourishing of critical and free thought. Such periods (which he sees as times of 'aggiornamento') existed not only in the West, but also in Muslim countries, until the religious authorities once again put a stop to them. Sadik al-Azm appeals therefore for a strict separation of religion and science, as the prerequisite for a dynamic society. That must be true, in his view, of Muslim countries as well.

The last speaker in the series was **Tariq Ali** *(Why are we so Obsessed by Islam?)*. Tariq Ali is a renowned writer and filmmaker. He is the author of an impressive series of works on world history and politics. He is also the editor of the *New Left Review*. It was primarily his much-celebrated work *The Clash of Fundamentalisms. Crusades, Jihads and Modernity* (London/New York, Verso, 2002), written shortly after the attacks of 9/11, that made him known to a wide audience around the world. In that book he placed the attacks in a broader historical perspective. The comments on his analysis were overwhelmingly positive at the time. Thus Anthony

Arnove (*The Nation*) wrote: "the book is an outstanding contribution to our understanding of the nightmare of history from which so many people are struggling to awake, and deserves serious engagement and consideration. Ali broadens our horizons, geographically, historically, intellectually and politically. … his mode of history telling is lyrical and engaging, humane and passionate". For Karen Armstrong, Tariq Ali's analysis reveals keenly how "self-interested and oil-greedy policies of the British and the Americans in such countries as Egypt, Israel, Saudi Arabia, and Iran … make our much-vaunted ideals of democracy and equity seem like a bad joke" (*The Times*). His contribution to this volume is introduced by Ludo Abicht, professor at the University of Antwerp and winner of the *Vrije Woord* (2005) prize, who situates Tariq Ali's work in its context. Ali's approach follows the same line as the critical analysis of Nasr Abu Zayd: he too points to the major role played by the Western powers in keeping Islam back: first by chasing Muslims from Europe, and then by systematically exploiting them during the period of colonialism. But Tariq Ali places more emphasis on the geo-strategic interests that come into play nowadays: via international capitalism, the systematic subjugation of Islamic societies simply continues. Over the centuries, there arose within these societies a great anger at the presence of foreign powers and at the corruption of their own elites who stood to gain from them. Such a situation has served in several countries as the breeding ground for the rise and success of Islamists. For Tariq Ali, the situation looks sombre. What continues to anger him is the obstinate stereotyping that goes on on both sides.

All seven lectures gave rise to stimulating discussion with the audience. Complete recordings were made of the debates with John Bowen, Bassam Tibi, Tariq Modood and Tariq Ali respectively. A selection of the most important questions in this volume may be found immediately after each of the papers. The questions give insight into the concerns of the audience: first of all, the desire that Islam should be compatible with a number of attainments of democracy and the rule of law, but also a strong interest in the burning question of the way in which these issues could best be addressed in the future: where does the responsibility of each lie? Can we as citizens make a contribution to the success of the multicultural society; how can we acquire reliable knowledge about Islam and what are the pitfalls of intercultural misunderstanding that we must do our best to avoid? Each discussion suggests commitment, both on the part of the ones raising the questions and on the part of the speakers, and above all the desire that over the long term we may succeed in understanding each other better. The

Introduction to The Anne & André Leysen Forum on 'Intercultural relations'

stumbling blocks have not been avoided: the accession of Turkey into the European Union, the falsification in history books of the relations between Islam and Europe, stubborn forms of mutual (cultural) racism, the weight of geo-strategic interests on a global scale, the relevance of the Palestinian question, the danger of political correctness, the risks of ghettoization in the big cities, etc.

The papers can of course shed only a certain amount of light on these problems, and each author necessarily speaks from his own experience. There is, however, a common message that comes through the seven texts in this volume. This message is that only *dialogue*, on the one hand between the West, that is, the countries that share the profile of a western democratic state governed by the rule of law, and Islam, but on the other hand also within the societies that have historically identified themselves as Muslim, will enable confrontation and negative animosity towards each other to make room for new possibilities: mutual understanding, free and critical thought and thus also social and community innovation. That, in turn, can lead to greater well-being. Undoubtedly there is still a long way to go before the conditions for an open dialogue between European countries and Islam, within and outside Europe, are fulfilled. And yet everyone shares a sense that it is on such dialogue that the future of our societies may well depend.

We acknowledge our debts to several people. The Forum benefited from a wonderful and supportive environment graciously offered by the Flemish Royal Academy of Sciences and Arts and from the support of Prof. em. Niceas Schamp in particular. The K.U.Leuven tradition of beneficence is Mrs. Isabel Penne's terrain of expertise, she and her assistants have saved no efforts to make it possible for us to set up the first A. & A. Leysen Forum. We also wish to thank, very warmly, Mrs. Betty Vanden Bavière and Mrs. Monica Sandor, who prepared the manuscript for publication. Their tremendous expertise, their accuracy, patience and sense of humor were much appreciated. And last but not least, Prof. em. Roger Dillemans, honorary rector of the K.U.Leuven played a major role in all this. To him this book is dedicated.

Marie-Claire Foblets
December 2007

Multiple Adaptations: Islam in Three Worlds

John Bowen

Throughout the early 2000s, Europeans read in their morning papers, at all too frequent intervals, of discords concerning the place of Islam in Europe: the Danes and their cartoons, the Pope and his views, the Germans and their Mozart. Many began to wonder whether Muslims and other Europeans could live together. Can Islam 'fit' into Europe?

I find this way of putting the question, about what Islam says or does or could do, to be the wrong way because it is socially ungrammatical. There is no Muhammad who speaks, not even a single written 'Islam' that reveals. What there is, what there has been, are millions of Muslims who read, speak, listen, and decide, largely about their everyday lives but also about questions of God and the Hereafter – just as do Christians, Jews, Buddhists and even some worried agnostics. I will argue here that the capacity of Muslims to adapt the texts and tenets of Islam to new institutions and values bodes well for Europe, but that their path is not and will not be an untroubled one. I also will claim that this path need not be one that passes by way of secularization and assimilation.

To lend some support to these claims I shall compare the ways some Muslims have adapted to new and changing conditions in the three places where I have some bits of knowledge: Indonesia, where I have worked since the late 1970s, the United States, where I live and teach, and France, where I have been studying the relationships of Muslims and non-Muslims for nearly a decade. In the contrasts lies a better understanding of the range of ways Muslims can fit institutions to local ways of life – but also the difficulties and questions thereby posed.

Institutional Logics

Indonesia

I begin with Indonesia precisely because it seems to pose no interesting questions at all. Long a Muslim-majority country, indeed the home of the world's largest Muslim population, and largely left to go its own way after it achieved independence after the Second World War, it would seem at first glance to have nothing to say about adaptations and integration. But a closer look tells a different story. Indonesian Muslims have been facing two challenges: how to construct a viable pluralistic yet religious society, with full recognition given to Christians, Buddhists, and so forth, and how to build and develop Islamic institutions without slavishly following Arabic culture. I will start with the second challenge and return to the first a little later on.

Beginning in the 15th century, traders and scholars began to bring Islam to various cities along the coasts of Sumatra, Java, and Sulawesi. They and the early local converts sought ways to adapt Islamic teachings to local ways of life. Most Indonesians were rural rice-growers, and, as in many such places, men and women worked together in the fields, married into one or the other's village, and used land there where they married. In some places men moved, in many more it was women, and in quite a few, such as where I worked in the highlands of Aceh, it could be the man or the woman who entered the spouse's village. After death or divorce, whoever remained in the village, man or woman, continued to use the land.[1]

In such a context, Arab-world Islamic property law made little sense. Rules that divided property among heirs by their gender (two shares to sons, one share to daughters, wherever they lived) were out of synchronization with the idea that land remains with those who stay in the village. Rules that give alimony to a wife after divorce but deny her a share of the household wealth makes even less sense in a place where wives might be effectively running the family farm and accumulating wealth. So they simply were not followed; local rules were.

After independence demand grew for uniform national laws regarding such matters, but it was only in the 1980s that the State called on Islamic jurists to develop an Islamic law code. They looked at Indonesia-wide practices and referred back to the whole history of Islamic law. Islamic jurisprudence or *fiqh* always was the product of judges and jurists drawing on the practices and values of Damascus or Fez, and on the norms to be found in the *Qur'ân* and in the words and deeds of Muhammad. By tacking back and forth between those sources of knowledge, the textual and the empirical, they arrived at decisions and created new norms – about contracts, or the way to build mosques, or what to say in prayer.

---

[1] For more on Islamic law in Indonesia, see Feener and Cammack (2007).

Drawing on these long-standing ways of fitting norms to local conditions, but within the boundaries set out in scripture, Indonesian jurists crafted a code of family law that responded to Indonesian ways of life. If Arab-world practices distinguished sharply between men's and women's worlds, Indonesian ones did not. Women and men worked together and therefore had relatively equal access to wealth, so jurists devised Islamic rules that divided all property acquired during a marriage, regardless of title, between the husband and wife. They also made husbands and wives appear before judges, should either wish a divorce, to justify that request. They preserved long-standing asymmetric categories of divorce: the husband still technically brings about a divorce by repudiating his wife, whereas a wife must appeal to a judge for an annulment. However, the conditions for both are the same: the husband, too, must have the judge's approval before he may pronounce the divorce formula.

Let me point to an interesting pay-off of the language used to develop these rules. Both those who believe in *fiqh* and those who believe only in international human rights and women's rights can find their positions realized in this code, at least partially. The rules draw from scripture and past Islamic scholarship, but they also move legal norms and practices toward gender equality.

This movement is not complete nor without challenge, but the point I wish to draw from the example is that in this Muslim-majority country Islamic authorities considered it necessary to reinterpret the texts and tenets of the religion to fit a developing national sense of gender equality. Conflicts of values and reinterpretation of religious norms is not uniquely characteristic of Muslims immigrating to Europe and North America.

France

Let me now turn to two such cases of recent immigration, France and the United States, and in both emphasize the adaptations Muslims have made to prevailing logic of State and religion, in public life, in the organization of mosques, and in the creation of schools.

Muslims are in France in relatively large numbers because of colonial labor policies. France recruited male workers from North and West Africa beginning in the late 19th century, long before other European countries. The incorporation of Algeria into France meant that it became the chief supplier of migrant labor among Muslim-majority countries. Although Portugal, Italy, and other European countries supplied many more immigrants before World War II, Algerian immigrants rose quickly in numbers during, and especially after the Algerian War, with migrants from Morocco and Tunisia next in numbers. (Portugal remains, however, the major place of origin for foreign nationals residing in France today, partly because Algerians take French citizenship in increasing numbers.)

Migrants were housed separately, near factories, and the initial spatial separation has been reproduced in subsequent generations, such that today Muslim immigrants or their children are more likely to live in poor neighbourhoods with high unemployment rates and poor-quality schools than are other immigrants, and much more likely than families of longer residence in France. They also are part of a very late coming to terms with the colonial past, with the tortures and felt betrayals of the Algerian War, the massacres of Algerians in France, and the treatment of non jazz-playing non-American blacks.[2]

Initially, governance of these residents was mainly a matter of colonial, not religious policy: Algerians and other Muslims in France, regardless of their nationality, were colonials, second-class citizens, controlled by labor bureaus and social welfare offices. But when and where the French State has recognized them as Muslims – in building the Paris mosque in the 1920s, and in efforts to construct a national Islamic organization beginning in the 1980s – they have done so in accord with long-standing patterns of State-religion relations.

Despite the generally-held notion that France is close to the ideal-type of a secularist system, with a strict separation of religions and State, in fact for centuries the French State has recognized, supported and thereby controlled its religions. Intimate involvement, not separation, is the real history of religion and State in France. This history begins in the 13th century and Philippe le Bel's creation of the 'Gallican Church', the arrangement whereby the King ruled the temporal dimensions of the Church while the Pope proclaimed doctrine. Napoleon's Concordat and his creation of national regulating bodies for the four recognized religions, the continuing role of these bodies after 1905, and the State's 2002-2003 creation of a national Islamic body, the CFCM, are evidence of this policy's continuity.

Muslims have indeed coalesced around this model, forming national-level associations and vying for seats on the directorship of the national CFCM. The State, for its part, has sought ways to

---

[2] On the history and sociology of the Muslim presence in France see Bowen (2008); Godard and Taussig (2007); Laurence and Vaisse (2004); and Silverstein (2004); on the debates about equality and diversity in France see Bowen (2007); and Shepard (2006). Kastoryano (2002) provides an important comparative analysis.

get around the constraints of the 1905 law that divested the State of churches, and the churches of direct public support. These ruses include the idea of creating a State Islamic university in Alsace-Lorraine (not governed by the 1905 law), subsidizing the secular portions of imam-training facilities, and encouraging mayors and prefects to work with local Islamic associations to build mosques and resolve problems of abattoirs.

These local collaborations have worked well there where the mayor views French law and policy in this way, and where a local Muslim entrepreneur is able to pull together diverse factions to agree on a mosque committee. I have been following this process most closely in the city of Bobigny, just north-east of Paris. There, mayoral advisor (and himself immigrant from Portugal) Jose Pinto cajoled Muslims into forming a united association to which the city could lease mosque land at 1 Euro per year. He is particularly concerned to ensure that Muslims do what he did – become good French citizens by following the rules. The key, according to Pinto, is that the building to which the city contributes is a municipal establishment, open to all and with some non-religious functions, while the act of worship itself remains none of the State's business. If French ideology urges religion to become private, French policy insists that the infrastructure of religion become public, thus controlled as well as subsidized – just as are cathedrals (maintained by the State) and many other churches (maintained by the local collectivities).

French schools also practice this dual logic of public and private. On the one hand, the universal school with a universal curriculum is the guarantor that children living in France grow up to be French in their thinking and acting and willingness to work together. On the other hand, and because such were the terms of the agreement between the Vatican and the State, everyone not only may opt out of this system by building private, confessional schools, but the State will pay their teachers' salaries. 40% of families in France have their children in one such school at one time or another.

Muslims are moving toward acquiring some of these resources. One or two private schools are close to being accepted by the Education Ministry as a 'private school under contract', teaching the national curriculum and accepting any eligible students, but giving an Islamic color to the school day – and having teachers salaried by the State.
They are doing so largely to give students better educations than what is available in their neighbourhood school.

I have been following classroom teaching in the most likely candidate for State recognition, in Aubervilliers north of Paris. I was particularly interested in how evolution was taught in science classes, and as it happens the teacher holds a doctorate in microbiology but wears a headscarf and therefore cannot teach in the public sector. She herself does not believe that humans and non-humans have a common ancestor but energetically teaches the national curriculum, focusing on the mechanisms of micro-evolution – and doing so in such a way that 100% of the school's students passed the *brevet*, the exam regulating passage from middle school to high school. Such an accomplishment is unusual in the district of Seine-Saint-Denis where the school is located, but was followed by the success some of these students had later on in gaining acceptance to good public high schools in better-off districts.

French Muslims' relative poverty has made them dependent either on international Islamic organizations or on the French State for assistance. But they also see participating in national associations, working with mayors to build mosques, and striving for State acceptance of Islamic schools, all as evidence of their civic engagement, a quality that they sometimes refer to by using '*citoyen*', citizen, as an adjective or adverb, as in 'a discussion that was very *citoyen*', or '*engagement citoyen*', a phrase that means something like 'with the interests of the community in mind.'

Often these phrases are uttered by people whose nationality is not French. I discussed these issues with Hakim el-Ghissasi, who has edited and produced magazines, web sites, and, as of 2006, television broadcasts on both sides of the Mediterranean, between his native Morocco and Paris, at the same time that he has been involved both in Moroccan politics and in working with mayors throughout France to promote community dialogue. When he discussed his engagements in France as *citoyen*, I asked him if his way of speaking meant that he had taken on French nationality. "Oh, these matters have nothing to do with papers," he replied.

As Hakim El-Ghisassi illustrates, the claim that one is *citoyen* may accompany a resolutely transnational mode of civic engagement. Many of those who come from North or Western Africa, for example, see themselves as deeply engaged civically in France and in their 'countries of origin'. They do not see these transnational engagements as lessening their degree of participation in France, though the state does see it that way (frequent travel counts against you when applying for papers). They are not a new form of 'transnational citizenship,' as some have suggested – no one practicing them discusses them in that way – but rather multiple engagements in national citizenship projects.

Muslims who see their activities as part of civic engagement do not, however, favor the use of the term '*intégration*'. They consider that term as implying that even if Muslims were born in France they must change to resemble more closely other Frenchmen and women. Where, they ask, is that written? Well, it is indeed part of the new 'contract of integration' that immigrants exchange old values for new ones, and the stakes in current policy struggles and resistance to deportations in France concern what precisely is meant by that language. Is long-term residence and enrollment in France evidence of integration, or are there other, less explicit criteria? I will return to this issue.

United States

Whereas Muslims in France are relatively impoverished and have retained active personal ties to countries of origins, Muslims in the United States are as a whole slightly richer than the national average and are less tied to international organizations. In part this relative autonomy is due to sheer physical distance: Pakistan is a lot farther from Chicago than Rabat is from Paris. But Muslims in the United States also had a clearer pathway toward integration to follow. Because most Americans see themselves as part of an immigrant story, the later arrivals fit right in. The major conflicts, at least before 9/11, were internal: between African-American Muslims, who had followed the very distinct religious path of Elijah Muhammad's Black Muslims until moving toward orthodoxy under his son, and immigrants, particularly well-off South Asians arriving after the 1960s, who brought a self-assurance about their superior understanding of Islam that matched the self-assurance that came from their social and economic standing. (today South Asians, Levant-origin Arabic speakers, and African-Americans are the major groups of Muslims.)[3]

The Muslims who came to the United States encountered a religious free market, with many churches competing for members, and with minimal regulation. A diffuse religiosity characterizes public life in the United States – it is nearly impossible to be elected to office if one states that one has no religious beliefs. Muslim immigrants thus had two pluses: they were immigrants in a society that defines much of its

---
[3] On Muslims in the United States see the essays in Haddad and Esposito (2000) and Leonard (2003).

past around immigration, and they publicly practiced their religion – in France a handicap but in the US an advantage.

But Muslims had one minus. They entered a land where conservative Protestants had a certain amount of weight in electoral politics and an ability to mobilize congregations for or against major public issues, especially moral ones. Some of those leaders urged their followers to consider Muslims as worshippers of a false god, i.e., whether or not they used the word, infidels.

The plethora of churches and other religious bodies in the US means that alignments and political power tend to be wielded not by specific denominations but by coalitions around values issues such as abortion, gay marriage, or science teaching in public schools. Thus Muslims joined conservative Christians in voting for George W. Bush in 2000 on these values issues, but turned against him in the 2004 election over the invasion of Iraq.

American responses to Muslims after 9/11 showed that the integration of Muslims, like politics, is very local. My family spends many summers in Colorado Springs, a bastion of Christian conservatism, and where the local imam had great difficulty weaving ties to local conservative ministers, and where after 9/11 some of these ministers emphasized the alien quality of Islam to Christianity. In Denver, by contrast, where imams had formed ecumenical organizations with Christians and Jews, churches by and large defended the religion of Islam and the civil rights of Muslims.

The absence of a formal structure governing US State-religion relations means that governances is mainly through the local religious institution – church, temple, or mosque, and this favors the emergence of more Congregationalist models of local religious governance, where the membership of the religious body pays for its upkeep and staff and controls its policies. As Jews and later Muslims migrated to the US their modes of governance adapted to this model. Mosques generally are financed by those who sign up as members, and a board elected by them chooses the imam.

All schooling is local in the US as well, an arrangement that produces a great deal of experimentation and innovation, but also inequalities between rich and poor school-funding districts. The relatively well-off position of immigrant Muslims means that they have found themselves mostly in well-off districts. Nonetheless, over 200 private Islamic schools exist in the US, most begun by immigrants.

In and around the city of Chicago are five private Islamic schools whose curricula are recognized by the State of Illinois (but receive no subsidies). Let me mention one, the Universal School, which opened its doors in 1990 and now has 600 pupils in primary and secondary levels. The school teaches the same subjects as public schools but adds Islamic Studies and Arabic for all pupils. Prayers are held twice daily. About one-half the pupils are from Pakistan. Islamic teaching emphasizes the general moral value of religious tenets, and indeed the school now uses a Moral Education curriculum developed for public schools – they teach the same materials and then add on a *hadîth* that supports the lesson, on honesty, for example.

If in France a discourse of civic engagement prevails across religions, in the US it is rather a discourse of moral values around which religious groups, and some non-religious groups, unite. That certain moral stances divide rather than unite – gay rights, or abortion rights – would make moral values particularly unsuited as a uniting rhetoric in France, where Republican universalism prevails, but works very well in the US, where no such universalism or unity is required by the prevailing logic of integration. This contrast in rhetoric corresponds to that of institutions as well: Muslims in France create Republican institutions that respond to national-level constraints and claim to act in the interest of national unity. Muslims in the US create religious institutions that respond to local-level demands and claim to act in the interest of (partially-) shared moral values.

Pebbles in the Shoe

If I have emphasized adaptation and integration it is to underscore the flexibility of institution-building, not to minimize the blocks. Whether they are stumbling blocks or road blocks we have yet to see. They arise from two sources: domestic pluralism and transnational structures of advice and control.

All countries are 'pluralistic' of course but each is in its own way. I have already signaled the major challenge posed for Indonesia: how to construct a viable pluralistic yet religious society, with full recognition given to Christians, Buddhists, and so forth. Indonesia grants distinct rights to its citizens depending on their declared confession. All Indonesians must state to which religion they adhere, and they must choose among a limited, albeit now expanded, list. Couples of mixed religion enormously complicate matters, of course, and have been the subject of extensive jurisprudence, but the broad idea is that Muslims have the right to have their cases decided under Islamic law. That this is seen as a right has to do with the colonial history of law; in 1937 the Dutch regime withdrew from those Islamic tribunals then in existence (primarily on Java and Madura) the right to adjudicate inheritance cases, leaving them with jurisdiction only over marriage and divorce. Many Indonesians remembered this slight long after independence, and they saw the creation of a nationwide Islamic court system in 1989 as a final assertion of independence.

Some groups wish to take things further and expand the domain of Islamic law. In 2006 the issue gripping the country is the rise, here and there and especially in Aceh, of laws and regulations seeking to 'enforce *sharî'a*' beyond the bounds of family law. Local officials in several cities have passed regulations that ban gambling, forbid women to be out by themselves late at night, or require restaurants to close during the fasting month. Most commentators agree that the politicians behind these regulations saw such measures as popular, given the local perception that the police cannot deal effectively with moral crimes, but one of Indonesia's two largest Islamic associations, the Nahdhatul Ulama, has opposed the regulations as undercutting national unity. In a special case having to do with long-running civil conflict, the province of Aceh is now permitted to base its laws and decisions on *sharî'a*.

Although the small groups calling for more Islamic law also highlight their transversal ties with Islamic groups elsewhere in the world, it would be a mistake to see Indonesian support for local Islamic law as mainly a local realization of 'globalized Islam'.

When mayors or officials of Aceh province called for development of laws based on *sharî`a*, they did so in the name of local rule and special characteristics. The official responsible for proposing *sharî`a* laws to the Acehnese Parliament justifies the laws as a return to Aceh's particular ways of life, its distinctive norms and values. For these groups and actors, *sharî`a* is a symbol of a return to self-governance, a final liberation from colonial rule. What it means for national unity or gender equality we have yet to see.

Trans-National Islam

Before turning to the matter of pluralism in France and Europe let me mention a second potential source of trouble for Islamic adaptations, one that stems from the universal character of norms in Islam.

Transnational networks or Muslim religious authorities located elsewhere, or even newly-arrived immigrants, may demand that Muslims in any one society remain consistent with what they claim to be an internationally valid set of norms. In a few mosques in the US, for example, recent immigrants from South Asia have accused current mosque leaders of 'laxism' or deviation. In Indonesia, the small groups seeking to expand the domain of Islamic law cite the positions taken by Saudi Arabian religious authorities to criticize positions taken by Indonesian ones.

Can Muslims adapt Islam to each society where they live if the highest authorities claim that, in the name of the universal *ummah*, there can only be one set of norms? Well, there are substantial resources within Islam that support pluralism. One is the long-standing acceptance among Sunni Muslims that the four major legal schools – the Hanafî, Hanbalî, Shâfi`î, and Mâlikî – all represent legitimate, if differing, ways to interpret scripture. Another is the idea that social necessity will lead Muslims to act differently in different environments. For example, generally-accepted rules prohibit Muslims from lending or borrowing at interest, but some Muslims living in Europe found this rule to run counter to the interests of their community. In 1999 some of these Muslims asked for a ruling from the European Council for *Fatwa* and Research, a collection of jurists of various nationalities, most of whom now reside in Europe. The Council is led by the highly influential Egyptian jurist Sheikh Yusûf al-Qardâwî, currently of Qatar. The Council replied in the form of a *fatwa*, in which they reaffirmed the prohibition on borrowing from banks that charge interest, and urged Muslims to devise alternative ways of financing homes, such as paying in installments, but also said that if they had no such alternatives, then they could take out a mortgage for a first house. They cited the doctrine of extreme necessity (*darurat*), which allows Muslims to do what otherwise is forbidden under compulsion, and said that in Europe renting keeps the Muslim in a state of uncertainty and financial insecurity. U.S. Muslims have followed suit.

Although the world of globalized or transnational Islam is almost always portrayed as having to do with spread of intolerant teachings, perhaps from Saudi Arabia, and incitements to *jihad*, in fact these developments, though real, are only part of the story. The other part is the access ordinary Muslims now have to multiple, and often conflicting, sets of interpretations and norms, and thus their capacity to choose as individual Muslims the path they see fit to follow. The globalization of information has facilitated the individualization of Islam.[4]

---

[4] For an important viewpoint in some tension with my own, in that it emphasizes sociological processes over internal Islamic reasoning, see Roy (1999).

France and Europe

But what of Muslims living in Europe? Is there only one set of 'correct' choices for individual Muslims in France or Belgium or Italy to make? Should we consider that the 'ideal European Muslim' is the 'Muslim by tradition', who does not practice very much, or does so at home, and perhaps does not believe very much either, and is almost indistinguishable on the street from other citizens – well, more so in southern France or Italy than in Denmark or Belgium – in short, the relatively 'invisible Muslim'? Or would we also accept as equally appropriate to Europe a devoutly worshipping, mosque attending, goat-sacrificing man with a short beard, or a woman with a black head scarf – in short, the 'visible Muslim'? Does successful adaptation or integration require Muslims to become invisible?

Now, there are reasons why one might say 'yes' to that question. Let me suggest some of them. First, some political theorists write that people who hold beliefs they hold to be infallible are less well suited to democratic life than those who do not, because they are less likely to change their views as an outcome of democratic processes of deliberation. If you hold that view, then all 'true believers' in Islam should be considered less suited for democracy than others, but so should 'true believers' in Catholicism or Protestantism, or for that matter true believers in free-market liberalism, or those who could not imagine putting European interests over national ones. All are ill-suited for democratic life under this view, and hence we must leave leadership to the doubters. I am not sure that any of us would subscribe to such an idea; we believe that people can strongly hold beliefs and yet be good democratic citizens.

A second, closely related claim regards living in society rather than participating in politics. Living together in society requires a good deal of openness towards others and general habits of sociability. Religious beliefs and practices that do not accord full respect and recognition to others – let us go beyond mere 'toleration' – are thus ill-suited to life in an European context. If Muslims believe that they are right and others wrong (about God, the afterlife, and so forth), then they fail this test, goes this claim. Like the first one, this claim sounds reasonable, but it would be difficult to criticize Muslims on this point and not criticize Catholics for thinking that Protestants' views on Christ are mistaken (or vice-versa). Indeed, I think that the supreme test of holding a religious view in a multi-religious society (as virtually all societies are) is to consider your own beliefs to be absolutely true while according civic respect and human respect to those who believe otherwise. How many of us would pass that test with flying colors?

Thirdly, the equality of men and women is a fundamental tenet of European societies, and yet some Muslims frown on too much mixing of the sexes, shaking hands, and so forth, and does not Islamic law discriminate against women? If they cannot accept complete equality and renounce Islamic law, they cannot be fully European. This argument may be the most sensitive of those I put forth here, and it seems to me to consist of two distinct concerns. One has to do with mixing: to frown on too much physical contact between men and women is to segregate, surely a bad thing to do. And yet at least in my own country there always have been girls-only schools, and they still command a great deal of respect for the freedom they give to girls to develop specific kinds of sociability among themselves. Most of the world's large-scale religions propose distinct roles for men and women, and some mandate celibacy as well. The most telling point to be made here regards what happens in public life, as when people shake hands, something a small number of Muslim women do not wish to do with men. (There have been a number of shocked editorials in France on this topic.) And yet, when someone balks from public kissing, the French way of greeting, do we automatically condemn that person for her or his lack of sociability, or simply note that people differ in the kind of physical contact they wish to have with members of the opposite sex?

The second concern focuses more pointedly on equality before the law and in public life more generally, and here is where the external evidence comes in, for example from Indonesia, where, as we saw, Muslim jurists, working in an all-Muslim context, have been able to shape Islamic law along relatively gender-equal lines. Do all Muslims accept these views? No. Are there areas of gender inequality? Yes; the possibility of taking more than one wife is one such area. But the important point is that these are matters of debate among Muslims, not a broad difference in values between 'Islam' and 'the West.' Many Muslim leaders, for example, argue that polygamy is not a right but a dispensation, and thus it is perfectly acceptable for a country to forbid it and then an obligation of Muslims to obey that law. Moreover, and here I refer to France, a country that prevented women from voting until 1945 and where the highest public officials routinely take mistresses is in a poor place to criticize Islam on these grounds.

So far I have considered several arguments for preferring the 'invisible' and perhaps not too observant Muslim to the 'visible' and more strictly observant one, arguments concerning political deliberation, sociability, and gender relations. I have argued that we already are capable of welcoming people with strong convictions and varying ideas about gender into the life of European democracies. But there is also a fourth objection which is not based on universal principles but on regional commonalities: that European societies have a common set of values and a shared look and feel, characterized by cathedrals, camembert, and chocolate, and that mosques, headscarves, and the sound of Arabic on the street just do not fit in.

Insofar as this objection concerns common values or heritage, it is difficult to square it with the centuries of bloody conflict that characterize European history – over religion, over labor rights, over rights to self-government and indeed over basic human decency. If there are 'common European values' they are in the general principles of equality and respect now enshrined in the European Convention on Human Rights: and that is a document to which Muslims living in Europe subscribe as well as do Catholics, Jews, and Protestants.

Insofar as the objection is to the presence of Islamic headscarves and mosques in European public life, we would all agree that the look and feel of everyday life in many parts of Europe has changed, in part because of growing free movement within Europe and indeed around the globe. We must also recall that it was European governments and captains of industry who incorporated parts of Asia, Africa, and the Americas into their empires, and then invited people from those lands to come to work in Europe.

Now, those doing the inviting probably made certain assumptions that have turned out not to hold. They assumed that the guests would leave at the end of the party (say, when recession hit in 1973). But it seems to me that this assumption was one that violated what Europe now holds to be a human right, the 'right to lead a normal family life', which is enshrined in the Convention and in many constitutions, and which gives residents the right to marry, have children, and bring their close relatives to live with them.

The powers that encouraged labor migration to Europe may have come to assume or predict or at least hope that anyone who stayed would privatize their religion, hide their beliefs, be the invisible Muslim I sketched out earlier, and leave public life to the cathedrals and the Christmas celebrations. But it seems to me that this assumption violates another right, the right to express one's religious beliefs that is equally enshrined in Europe's fundamental documents. The notion that it is up to non-Muslim Europeans to issue *fatwa*'s about what Muslims should wear or eat or believe is an astounding usurpation of this right. That one demands that everyone in Europe work toward realizing principles of equality is a duty as well as a right. That one demands that one worship at home rather than in a mosque, or dress as do the latest fashion models rather than as one's values dictate, is an instance of cultural arrogance. If we all share universalistic values, then we must apply them in a universalistic manner, and equally to all.

But this last issue, that Muslims have changed the landscape of Europe, does, I think, pose Europe's great challenge for this new millennium. The challenge is more difficult in places where in the past people tended to look and act alike – I am thinking of Denmark, Sweden and Norway, where xenophobia has its greatest hold – or in places where the sins of the Third Reich have not been fully recognized and expunged – I am thinking of Alsace, the current center of French anti-Semitism, and other realms of neo- (and not so neo-) Nazi sentiment – or in places where politicians seize on the electoral boost that anti-immigrant slogans can bring them – and of course I am thinking of Italy's Northern League, France's National Front and its imitators among the center-right UMP, and the Vlaams Belang in Belgium. This challenge is not just about Muslims in Europe; it is also about Jews in Europe and the handicapped in Europe and the very idea of Europe as a place for free movement, free exchange of ideas, and the fullest respect for all that is our common humanity. That is a challenge to which Muslims and non-Muslims, believers and skeptics, can, and must enthusiastically, embrace.

References

Bowen, J. R. (2007). *Why the French Don't Like Headscarves: Islam, the State, and Public Space.* Princeton: Princeton University Press.

Bowen, J.R. (2008). *Can Islam be French? Knowledge, Norms, and Sacrifice in a Secularist State.* Princeton: Princeton University Press.

Feener, M.R. & Cammack, M.E. (eds.). (2007). *Islamic Law in Contemporary Indonesia.* Cambridge: Harvard University Press, for the Islamic Legal Studies Program, Harvard Law School.

Godard, B. & Taussig, S. (2007). *Les musulmans en France, courants, institutions, communautés: un état des lieux.* Paris: Robert Laffont.

Haddad, Y.Y. & Esposito, J.L. (2000). *Muslims on the Americanization Path?* Oxford: Oxford University Press.

Kastoryano, R. (2002). *Negotiating identities: States and immigrants in France and Germany.* Princeton: Princeton University Press.

Laurence, J. & Vaisse, J. (2004). *Integrating Islam: Political and Religious Challenges in Contemporary France.* Washington, D.C.: Brookings Institution Press.

Leonard, K.I. 2003. *Muslims in the United States: The State of Research.* New York: Russell Sage.

Roy, O. (1999). *Vers un islam européen.* Paris: Esprit.

Shepard, T. (2006). *The Invention of Decolonization: The Algerian War and the Remaking of France.* Ithaca: Cornell University Press.

Silverstein, P.A. (2004). *Algeria in France : transpolitics, race, and nation.* Bloomington: Indiana University Press.

Questions and Answers

Q. My question relates to changes in Indonesia over the last twenty years, and in particular to characteristics of Islam. Is it now dominant, is there more familiarity with Arabic, is there a change in the percentage of Muslims, are there any social conflicts coming from islamization, and what about the role of women, the emancipation of women within Islam?

A. This of course is a wonderful set of questions, some of which I already addressed, or briefly addressed. It's true, Indonesia is a place that shows, along with Bangladesh, India and Pakistan – those are the four largest Muslim populations in the world – that Arabic societies, languages, institutions, are not synonymous with Islamic societies, languages, institutions, even though of course the *Qur'ân* is, from a Muslim perspective, the gift of God to Muslims, after the gift and the revelations given earlier to other prophets, such as Moses, Jesus. Arabic retains an importance that is comparable to Hebrew as practised by Jews: the study of Hebrew so that they are able to recite from the Torah is part of becoming a *Bar Mitzvah*, adult boy or girl, man or woman. Similarly there's always been an ability to read, memorize and recite *Qur'ân*, even in villages people will know how to recite a great deal of the *Qur'ân* from an early age, without necessarily understanding the meaning of the sentences. There has been some increase in Arabic literacy, but that general situation remains as before. One of the great controversies in Islam is about the status of translations of the *Qur'ân* into local languages. The arguments in favour are the obvious practical ones, while the arguments against are that these local versions delude or even betray the original character of the *Qur'ân*, which was that the Arabic was the proof of revelation of the direct contact between humans and God, for the human being Mohammed, who, was illiterate, could not have created these things himself. The compromise was that the translations are called 'commentaries', or 'interpretations' of *Qur'ân*, not direct translations.

Q. Are there parallelisms between critical Islam in India and Europe?

A. North India has been the most prolific source of many different streams of Islam, all the way from the very modernist to people who travelled around the world to bring Muslims back to the correct practice of Islam in a basic way, to the people who later became the

Taliban in Afghanistan. So a whole range. Northern India is also the area with the most divisions, the most opposition between schools not very far the one from the other, it's an extremely interesting area. But it did produce important reformist thinkers about Islam, who then influenced thinkers in Egypt and elsewhere and whose ideas later came to Europe and have been a source of important knowledge. Finally, there is a question I think I've touched upon to great extent. It's the question of how can it be that in societies where there is a separation between church and state, one can have Muslims and Islam becoming really a part of this society. In my view, the basic principles of separation are good ones, they're valid ones. There's no need for France or any other society to change its basic structure and way of thinking about things in order to integrate and make people feel at home. To the contrary! Some Muslim teachers whom I know have said: "you know, *laïcité*, if you take this to be the rules of the game in France, these are perfectly acceptable rules. We can work with these. The challenge is for people in France, and mutatis mutandis for people elsewhere in the world, to apply these equally and fairly to everybody."

Q. *My question relates to your plea for tolerance and respect for other cultures, other religions. I think most people would fully endorse that. But how would you more practically handle these real conflicts between, on the one hand, the imperative of tolerance and respect, and on the other hand intolerance of values which we hold so important, indeed like free speech. To put it in a very concrete way: if you were a newspaper publisher and had to make a decision after what happened in Denmark, would you publish these cartoons in your newspaper? What decision would you take? Would you publish the cartoons, with the risk of maybe needlessly offending a large Muslim community, and inflaming an already volatile situation? That's the trade. Or would you bow to pressure and start accepting restrictions on the free speech that we hold very dear? How would you have made that trade off? How would you have made that decision?*

A. Thank you for the question. Generally and specifically I think we need to think about both norms for publication and free speech and norms that Muslims follow. We need to understand conventions that are characteristic of other parts of the world. As I understand various European norms about publication, there are in fact some limits to free speech. If I were, in Germany or in France, to stand up and say there was no Holocaust, I'd be thrown in jail. There's a good reason for that law. If I were to stand up in France and say to somebody that, because he's a Muslim, he's a creature of the devil, I'd be put in jail, this is a public figure. Apparently if you call Islam a gutter religion you can win your case. Michel Houellebecq did that and was let off. He won his case. It's kind of a difficult border to define exactly. You are Europeans and I come from elsewhere. Because of your memories of the tremendous conflicts between communities that you've suffered through, over the centuries you've worked out some solutions, and developed new institutions out of these in an attempt to prevent further such conflicts. You've developed a great deal of sensitivity to the balance between free speech and guaranteeing a public peace. A sort of civic space where people can feel free to speak, rather than feeling that they will be attacked in their very being if they dare to enter that public space. I have great respect for that, I think that's very important and you should continue to reflect on that sort of balance. Clearly, the norms in France, the norms in Denmark, the norms in the UK are very different, because Europe is a very new creation. Europeans now have to find out what common norms ought to be. It's a matter of law, but it's also a matter of cultural practice. Of course within France there's no common value, you have on the one hand these harsh laws, and on the other hand there is the case of Charlie Hebdo, a publication that's delighted in skewing any religious figure that's profoundly and explicitly anti-religious and that inherits the tradition of terribly anti-Semitic and anti-Catholic cartooning. Now is that something you want to defend? I'll leave the question up to you. I would dodge your question, no I would not have published those.

Q. *I have two questions. The first relates to the degree of acceptance determined by the speed of immigration. There is a German theory - all theories come from Germany of course - a German theory that says that you can go to a certain level of immigration and then you get trouble anyway. The second question is whether you see the Muslim world as a unity? I've been told that Turks and Arabs are completely different people, is that correct? Because it is so important for us, as you must know, I see the question of what we do about Turkey from a political point of view. If we let Turkey into the European Union we get a completely different picture. We get half of the Muslim world, and that could lead to a new split. In case there is indeed unity between the Arabs and the Turks, then we are in for trouble.*

A. There certainly has been a great deal in the sociology of immigration about the levels of toleration a society has, or that even a housing project or a neighbourhood has. In the US there's a similar literature about African-Americans, blacks and whites. Very similar ideas. Well, I would have two sorts of answers to that. The first answer would be to say: 'is that the question you want to lead with? Or do you want to lead with the question of what European policy and norms and rights about immigration and integration should be? The second answer is less dodging: the question is that it's a matter of immigrants, it's not even a matter of waves of immigration with a first, second and third generation. Looking at the post-World War II era, what you get are, from each of the major countries, different moments when there are pushes of immigrants, and other moments when there are fewer; and these can be totally different populations. Looking at Tunisians, there's a very educated group coming at one moment, there's a much less educated group of workers coming at another, and then of course some of these people go back, some of them stay and have children. So if you look at a school outside Paris, consisting largely of immigrants, as some have, you'll have people of the same age who've just come, whose parents came, whose grandparents came, or even whose great-grandparents came. So who are they? At what point do they become no longer immigrants, but people born there and therefore full citizens as well as nationals? That then becomes a question of how people in the rest of the society perceive them, and that's where it gets quite complicated. I wish we had much better studies of immigration in Europe, that would get over the idea of there being a simple first, second and third generation story, as if it only happened once, as if everybody came in 1962 and then it stopped.

As to the second question, let me draw a parallel: how unified is Europe and how distinct are your countries? Of course the question depends on "about what?". Similarly, if Muslims in Indonesia and Muslims in Tunisia and Muslims in Turkey come together and talk about translations of the *Qur'ân*, or they get together and they pray, they're all practising the same religion, there may be a slight difference in the way their fingers and hands are positioned, but these are non-essential differences. If they get together and talk about the place of Islam in public life, or the proper role of women in society, then they might start to have bigger differences. And then, if they talked about foreign policy or with whom they ought to unite at the UN on a certain issue, then the alliances will be determined by totally other issues. So to come back to your Turkey question, maybe you're suggesting I get to decide at this moment "is Turkey in or out?". It certainly is a complicated question, as complicated for Turkey as it is for people already within the European Union. But your question was how much would Turkey become part of a huge block of Arab Muslim countries. I don't think that there's an alliance of all countries that have large Muslim populations against countries that have a Christian population.

Q. *At times, creativity offers the best solution. Let me give you an example. I am working in a hospital. Out of five assistants, three are women. One of them comes from Bosnia, she claimed the right to dress traditionally, i.e., in black and with the headscarf. Since we do not accept any exception to the rule, her claim was dismissed. In practice, however, there seems to be no insurmountable problem: this woman eventually conformed to the rules. The doctor's uniform indeed proves sufficiently respectful of her own dress code: her hair is covered, her body wrapped in a spacious pinafore.*

A. I completely agree. I think we have to address problems both in a pragmatic way and with due regard to general principles. By general principles I mean the principles of European life, that need to be taken universalistically, that was the point of my talk. I completely agree that the solution really lies in these local compromises. I mentioned the case in France of the local municipal counsellor working with a Muslim group, who defined the right to have the mosque built with State help. Paris is going to spend an enormous sum of money to build two buildings in the eighteenth arrondissement. These buildings will be given to Islamic cultural associations, not religious, that can then rent them to Islamic religious associations to become mosques. We're getting around, so there's a lot good will to arrive at these compromises. For example, in my book on the history of the French debate about headscarves, I write that I find it unfortunate that it was made into a national debate, when there were very few cases. In fact in many schools, including the ones I know quite well, the principal had worked out compromises with those two or three girls who wanted to wear headscarves. The bandana or something, very much like your case, so I agree.

Q. *Isn't there a difficulty with this kind of practical solutions? They lack legal certainty. You never know in advance what will be the outcome, even when the case is very similar. So what remains of the requirement of legal certainty in such a case-by-case approach? And in addition, I think there is no lack of willingness on the part of the majority society to adapt and to find solutions, but there is a lack of knowledge about what within Islam is the right or the correct view. So how would you address that very specific difficulty? Where do you find the necessary data that can guarantee a solution that is in conformity with Islam?*

A. Well of course in the law as in the day-to-day life of schools and workplaces, we're always making case-by-case decisions and compromises. How do we decide what's in the best interest of the child? We look at lots of factors. A school teacher in France in 2002 would look at lots of factors. It reminds me of a girl who wore the headscarf in a way and seemed to participate entirely in school affairs. The principal was of the opinion that her behaviour was within the margin of tolerance, this woman was fully a part of the school life. Another person who wore a black complete head covering and refused to participate seemed to the professor to be sending a message of separateness. There has to be sort of an attitude of participation. How would you measure that? As to the second part of your question, whom do you ask, if you're a State official, about what Islam says? And of course the problem is that there is no such thing that all Muslims will agree over. You're absolutely right, you have to find that knowledge, and the way you do it then must depend on the way in which each country best carries out its relationships with Islam.

Q. *The question relates to the capacity of Muslims to adapt the text and tenets of Islam to our basic values, or to fit in with our basic values. You write in your paper: "I wish to challenge those who believe it lies with secularisation and assimilation." Don't you think this getting together can only succeed in an equilibrium between, on one hand, respect for their religious authenticity, for their cultural identity, and on the other hand, our values, our institutions, the state of law in Europe which has been developed over the years? Therefore I think your statement should be balanced, it should be both of them, some respect for their part of what we consider our basic values should also be put on the agenda. Schooling and education can play a very* *important role in that. It's not one or the other, it should be one and the other.*

A. Thank you, because the whole purpose of beginning that way was to indeed challenge people who say "yes, there are basic values", to challenge my statement. I would have two responses. One would be: we have to look at which element we're talking about, certainly the element of basic human rights, gender equality, all those enshrined in legal documents, those are elements of our basic framework for living together. There's no reason to change those and there's nothing about Islam that prevents Muslims from perfectly adhering to those basic legally defined rights. But if we say gay marriage, it depends on the country. Is there a common European value of gay marriage? Does every European agree gay marriage is a good thing? There's a continuum. So I think we have to look at exactly what we are talking about. Communism? Socialism? Where are the values exactly? Freedom of speech we discussed, we can come back to it, but the general point is we have to ask precisely about what we are speaking.

Q. *I have two questions: the first is about values, since you addressed the issue of European values. A few months ago I bought, here in Brussels, at the North station, a newspaper edited by homeless people: they are very grateful to the Muslim community in Belgium for having helped them during the winter months. So there are values in Islam which they feel are not so present in our society, such as for example beneficence and prayer. It is quite important to remember the day-to-day contacts: not only do we look at them, but they also look at us. The second question relates to memories on both sides. Islam has been in Europe for thirteen centuries, it's not a new story. It's an old story with clashes. In Hungary, you hear Hungarian people speaking of the whole range of churches and cloisters and monasteries that were destroyed during 150 years by the Ottomans. In Greece, you hear Greek Muslims complaining that their whole culture was destroyed after 1830. The same is going on today with Kosovo, with the Serbian monasteries and churches, it's going on in the Caucasus, with Chechnya, etc. How do you feel about this dimension of history in Europe? What in your view are the possibilities today for healing these memories, not only on an academic discussion level, but also in concrete ways? Because one of the great things we lack in Europe is hospitality.*

A. I was enjoying your comments rather than thinking of answers. There was very rich testimony to the variety of memories, and yes, Europeans have long memories that can be drawn on for the good or the bad. Indeed one of the great struggles in many parts of Europe today is to work through more recent memories. In France it's only now that the Algerian war becomes a topic for open discussion. In my view, it is going to be a more important healing process through public debate for Muslims currently in France than our longer-term memories. For Greece and Hungary I have nothing to say except that you're bringing this up. I don't believe that an adequate solution for a local or a civil conflict is ever, in the long term, memory of a past conflict. All too often during the beginning of the dissolution of Yugoslavia the Ottoman history was brought up, and indeed there were people in Yugoslavia that were citing this and that value from the fourteenth century, yes, but is that the memory that drove them to kill each other in the first place? It facilitated religious differences but also ethnic difference. Rwanda was not about religion, Rwanda was mobilization on the basis of ethnicity. Ethnicity, language, religion, other sorts of easily seizable differences that can be mobilized by people if they wish to carry on a particular action of secession, killing other people, wiping out the opposition, whatever it may be, and that's always been the case.

Q. *I want to return to your text and touch the core question: integration. "For centuries European values have been warlike attitudes towards each other" was your observation. And then I ask myself why do you say that? The answer cannot simply be that you have to give Muslims the time, because then you're implying that "if you Europeans have solved all these problems and have invested a long time in doing that, well maybe Muslims will as well", and then your real ideal must be the invisible Muslim, because you're giving examples which show that Catholics have also effaced themselves. "We don't pray on the streets, we have done away with all those things, well, Muslims will do like that". Your preference is for the invisible Muslims.*

A. There's an empirical question and a normative question in your observation. The empirical one is "is a good European one whose religion is never let on in public". While I worked in the last couple of years, I was struck how Jean-Pierre Raffarin as soon as he had become prime minister started emphasizing his regular church-going habits. In Ireland, on the contrary, people consider their religion to be none of anyone's business and to have nothing to do with their public affairs The secularization that I'm seeing in Europe isn't one of either ceasing to believe strongly in the superiority of my beliefs over and against yours about God, or whatever it might be. Hans Küng of course can say what he wants, but there are plenty of people who believe one version of religion and do not think that the others are going to be saved, just leaving aside Islam for a moment. Secularization is a process of the construction of ways for people to get along in the public sphere and in political life. So I don't see secularization as necessarily implying invisible Muslims. Do you allow the mosques to be there, do you allow the public display or the public observance of Islam, as most women who wear headscarves would talk about it, through a headscarf, just as one would allow the cross or other signs of religion? I think that's the issue. A part of this is, I would agree with you on certain of these points, for example: it did take France until 1945 to give women a vote, but they did it, so that's over, fine, and so now we give Muslims more time. I think that may be a valid point. It's sort of a cheap trick to say "okay, the four largest Muslim countries have all had female heads of state", it's a little cheap because they're all related to men in one way or another, but it's not so clear to me that when you start to look at the compositions of some of those parliaments, you don't find gender balances.

Q. *Visibility is of course also symbolic. In a way you said: "wearing the beard, wearing the anorak, wearing this, wearing that might be a sign for many Europeans of the non-acceptance of the local situations they find here, in the country that accepts them, that receives them". That's one kind of visibility, of course. Do you think that this visibility prevents integration?*

A. Well of course that's very tricky, because we're talking about several levels of semiotics, right, or signification. We're talking of what, say, a person on the street seeing a woman in a headscarf thinks that woman is intending, and I'm not sure what we think about that. Those semiotics vary much from one country to another. Then we're talking about what we as analysts think that woman is intending by her very wearing of that headscarf. How do we know? There's of course a range of such intentions. And then we have to ask: what do we think about taking either that woman's report of what she intends, which may or may not be what she really does, and taking the report by the other person on the street, the non-Muslim, of her or his reaction. What do we make of all that? Do we make of that: "well, if you enlisted a negative reaction by wearing such and such, then you shouldn't do it", or do we say "we all have something to learn here about accepting the existence of that other side"? Let me go back to the school superintendent of that one school in France. Whether I agree or not with her particular stance on headscarves, it was nonetheless one that tried to differentiate between different kinds of headgear in terms of the message she thought was being communicated to the other students by one sort of headgear as opposed to another. So she was responding to what you said, that it's the display of a willingness or an unwillingness to become part of that group that is the most important issue. I think we have to be careful in taking perhaps the most negative reactions to a particular sign as the basis for public policy. But in general I would agree with you that it is these intentions to become part of the society that are critical.

Q. Recent studies show that Flemish adolescents feel threatened by Islam. These young girls and boys, born in a multicultural society and who have access to numerous sources of information and data collecting, appear to be afraid. The same applies to elderly women: by experience I know how difficult it is, in practice, to make Flemish women and women of migrant origin meet with one another. None of them appear to be interested in the other. You are an anthropologist: what are, in your view, the reasons for this mutual lack of interest, which may even hide very negative feelings toward each other. It's a crucial issue. In my view we need to know one another, that is particularly true in the case of young people since genuine interest in one another's cultural background is a condition if our endeavour is to apply the insights your are supporting in your analysis.

A. What you were saying is that there really isn't any "*multiculturele samenleving*" [multicultural society], because "*het leven*" [life] isn't "*samen*" [together], it's just *next to* each other. There has been research for a long time about what used to be called "the contact hypothesis". The contact hypothesis claims that the more people come into contact with each other, the more they get used to each other, accept each other, even maybe like each other. It turns out that it's not true when put that way. A lot of this research was concerned with blacks and whites in the US, but also with other groups in different parts of the world. The best summary of the findings from these studies seems to be that, when there is contact that involves working together for a goal: yes. So sport fits in. People are trying to work together to win a game, or solve a problem in a factory, or solve anything else, as long as it's something outside of normal everyday life, or something in a church or whatever you can find. If they're trying to do something and they have to work together: yes. But if they simply come into contact, indeed stereotypes maybe reinforced. Now I see Jean-Pierre every day and I say "yeah, I used to have these stereotypes against people who wear black shirts with their sport cults, and now I know I really dislike these people because I see him and he confirms every one of my stereotypes". So it isn't true that just seeing people leads you to accept them. Local level institutions that involve cooperation, some sort of activity, are going to be necessary to break down these boundaries.

Q. *You didn't say a word on a number of troublesome issues: what is your response to the observation that young pious Muslims have started putting some pressure upon young girls, in particular, for the simple reason that these girls in their view do not behave in conformity with Islam, for example because they do not wear the headscarf?*

Q. *And what about the growing tensions between different communities of migrant origin? There is not only a problematic gap between the majority society and newly immigrated groups, but also among migrants themselves. Yet another alarming observation is the fact that the language skills of youngsters of the third generation are manifestly less well developed than the skills of boys and girls of the previous generation. Language is a main tool, it enables one to acquire new knowledge. We need to make of these people full citizens.*

A. I won't say much at the end, because we're drawing to a close. I think that the issue of freedom, of liberty, that you raise, is one of the key ones. And I think it's important, though this would be a sort of general concern, to relativize, or to place next to other cases, the case of Muslims. Because of course we want parents not unduly to force their children to do things they really don't want to do, but of course we also encourage parents to guide children. And when a Catholic parent brings a child to Catholicism and makes sure that a child follows that route, or becomes a lawyer or a judge as she or he did, we see no reason to worry. But when it is to go to the mosque, maybe we have a different response. So we have to ask whether we are concerned with the degrees of pressure or the particular content of that pressure. Each time we think about Muslims, we ought to say: "well let me think about another kind of case and see if that changes the way I think about that". And of course there are legal limits and definitions placed on the ability and powers of fathers and mothers to shape what their children do and to place undue pressure on them. So of course I respect the importance of guarding the freedom of girls and boys to explore their identities, indeed this is what schools encourage them to do, the French school particularly. I think that's a very valuable role, but what I wouldn't want to do is make the assumption that every time we see a girl or a woman wearing a headscarf we assume it's because someone has told her to do it. What does that say about our belief in women's agency with respect to men's? There may be cases like that, but there are many, many other cases that are not at all like that. Putting on a headscarf is part of an effort to distance oneself from one's parents, or to justify one's work life with respect to one's old-fashioned mother, or because one really wants to live a life in religious terms. We have to credit the possibility that some people really believe in religion. And there may be many other sorts of possibilities including pressure from a local, that's also possible, but we have to ask ourselves what we really know about the tensions and the background and history of something that we see, and not the whole "I know why, because they all do it this way". That's something we would never accept about our own community, and we shouldn't expect Muslims to accept it about theirs either. The more we have people like Marie-Claire Foblets and others, leading teams of researchers to discover more about the way in which newcomers to the society are or are not fitting in, what their interpretations are, the better armed we will be, as you were pointing out quite rightly, knowing better the reasons behind what they're doing, in order to truly welcome them in and truly measure their efforts to become full members of the society.

Professor Bowen. I'd like to just thank you for the opportunity not only to address you – I hope there was some usefulness in it – but also to you for all the probing and important questions you posed and for this chance to have this discussion with you tonight. And again to Marie-Claire Foblets, to the academy and to the family that made this all possible. Thank you very much.

Professor Foblets. I take two points from this meeting. First, in Europe it seems we underestimate the potential for adaptation on the part of the Muslim communities among us.

And the second point, maybe we also underestimate the responsibility that weighs upon our shoulders, because part of the problem are our own perceptions, the way we perceive things. It may well be that we add to the difficulties by sticking at our own views and by not sufficiently problematizing them. I think these are two main insights. Let's take them with us to the next meetings in this series.

The Poldermujahidin:
The Radicalization of Young Dutch Muslims

Ruud Peters

Introduction

With the murder of the filmmaker and publicist Theo van Gogh by a young Dutch Muslim, the Dutch became acutely aware of the presence in their midst of a groups of radicalized Muslims, some of whom were willing to use violence. Not much is known about their ideas. In this essay I will describe the process of radicalization from within, by analyzing the writings of Mohammed Bouyeri, the murderer of van Gogh. This is based on the report I wrote as an expert witness for the court where he was tried. Bouyeri was sentenced to life imprisonment.

I will start with a short survey of Dutch Islam. We have to bear in mind, however, that the number presented here are based on the religious situation in the countries of origin, since Dutch population registration does not include information of religious affiliation. Thus, these numbers on the one hand include persons from Muslim majority countries, who have given up their religion and on the other hand exclude Dutch converts. According to the latest estimations of the CBS (Central Bureau of Statistics)[1], there are about 850.000 Muslims in the Netherlands. Their origins vary enormously. About 600.000 of these are of Moroccan and Turkish origins. The first generations of them came to the Netherlands as labour migrants; many others came as family members of the first generation, or were born in the Netherlands. Another substantial group of over one hundred thousand are those who arrived as refugees from countries like Iraq, Iran, Afghanistan and Somalia. The distribution of Muslims over the country is unequal: In the large cities they constitute between 15 and 20% of the population, against a national average of 5%.

---

[1] *NRC-Handelsblad*, 24-10-2007.

Van Gogh's Murderer and His Ideas

When immediately after the murder of Theo van Gogh Mohammed Bouyeri was arrested, the police found out that he had around him a small group of some ten or fifteen like-minded youngsters. They did not form a tight organization; its members used to visit on an irregular basis gatherings in Bouyeri's living room, where they discussed religion and exchanged digital documents with religious and radical Islamist contents. The police investigation and subsequent trial did not reveal any direct organisational links with international Islamist terrorist groups. The 'Hofstadgroep', as they became to be known, is, therefore, an example of home-grown Islamic extremism. However, during the initial stages of the radicalization period, a certain Abu Khaled Redouan el-Issa, a former Syrian army officer who had applied for political asylum in Germany, played a role by introducing them to the thought of Sayyid Qutb (1906-1966) and Abu al-A`lâ al-Mawdûdî (1903-1979), the founding fathers of Islamic radicalism.

At the time of the arrests of Bouyeri and members of the group around him the police seized their computers. As an expert witness I had access to the data. One of the things I did was to identify Bouyeri's writings. I found about sixty texts produced by him. Some were Dutch translations of Islamists pamphlets or treatises, often preceded by a short introduction by Bouyeri. Other texts were entirely written by himself. With one exception the source texts of the translations were in English. It seems that Bouyeri's knowledge of Arabic was not sufficient for translating complicated religious treatises. The texts he produced were distributed among the other members of the group and some of them were published on the internet. Evidently, Bouyeri was the ideological leader of the group and his texts were, it seems, used for ideological training. Apart from his texts the computers contained enormous libraries of religious written material, most of it in Arabic, as well as pictures and short video movies. Most of the latter were related to the oppression of Muslims in e.g., Palestine/Israel, Chechnya, Iraq and Afghanistan, and their armed struggles against oppression. The videos were probably used for recruitment, in order to convince potential members of the plight of Muslims all over the world and the need to do something about it.

An inventory of the documents found on his and other computers shows that he and the group were ideologically heavily indebted to the Egyptian Sayyid Qutb and the Indian/Pakistani Abu al-A`lâ al-Mawdûdî. Moreover large amounts of more recent Salafi material, especially from radical Saudi religious scholars and from authors who had fought in Afghanistan were found. Among Bouyeri's translations we find a few texts originally written by radical Saudi scholars and by Afghan *jihad* veterans. However, the impact of one figure stands out: Abu Hamza al-Misri (b. ca. 1957), the militant imam and preacher of the Finsbury Mosque in London. Born in Egypt, he immigrated to England in 1979. In the early 1980s he fought with the Mujahidin in Afghanistan where he lost his hands and an eye. Bouyeri translated quite a few of his writings, via English versions, into Dutch.

The Construction of a Dutch Extremist Islamist

On the basis of the document properties of Bouyeri's texts I could establish the chronological order in which they were produced. This enables me to track the process of radicalization which they went through. Within this process we can distinguish four stages:
- Explicit rejection of Western values and norms
 (starting February 2003)
- Rejection of Western democracy and law (as of October 2003)
- Global call for *jihad* against democracy (March 2004)
- Justification of violent actions and the writing of threatening letters
 (Summer 2004)

'The quest for the truth'

The beginnings of Bouyeri's radicalization can be dated back to the year 2001. In the Summer of that year he had served a prison sentence for assault and battery. Later he said that in prison he had started to read the *Qur'ân*. His need for a new spiritual orientation was given a new impetus with the death of his mother in December of that year. In the testament drawn up by him shortly before he killed van Gogh, he mentioned that after his mother's death in December 2001 he set out on a 'quest for the truth.' That his ideas and behaviour changed during the following year is well documented by testimonies of friends and colleagues.[2] He became more serious and religious. In his work – he had dropped out of college and found a part-time job as assistant-manager of a community centre in his neighbourhood – he began to take Islamic injunctions more seriously: he refused to order alcoholic

---
[2] The best biographical account is to be found in Jutta Chorus and Ahmet Olgun, *In godsnaam: Het jaar van Theo Van Gogh*. Amsterdam: Contact, 2005.

drinks for receptions and parties and to organize activities where men and women would mingle.

Against the ensuing criticism he defended himself in a short article published in the centre's magazine in February 2003 and entitled: 'Islam and integration.' This I consider as the first step on the path of radicalization. Whereas the Dutch public debate at that time was dominated by the question of whether or not Islam is compatible with integration into Dutch society, Bouyeri turned the question on its head by positing that the only true integration was integration into Islam:

> The verb integrating means ... becoming part of a larger whole. This includes for me the Islamic concept of submission (body and soul) to the Unique Power who is the Creator of the larger whole that we call universe and of which man is part.

This, he argues, imposes on him the duty of following Islamic prescriptions, even if these are in conflict with prevailing views in society. At that time he was still searching for the true Islam. Gradually fundamentalist notions become more prominent in his translations and writings. This was the result of two events. The first one was that the authorities did not accept his proposal for a social club for Moroccan youth. Assisted by the community centre where he was employed he had put a great deal of energy and lots of time in the application government funding. When his plans were rejected, he felt frustrated. He saw it as evidence that Dutch politicians did not take Muslims seriously and his trust in the Dutch political system and Dutch society in general was shaken. The other event was that his contacts with the Syrian preacher Abu Khaled el-Issa intensified. Bouyeri and his friends had met him in one of the Amsterdam mosques in the previous Fall, but El-Issa began to visit and teach them sometime during the Spring of 2003. In the Summer of that year documents were distributed among the members of the group consisting only of *Qur'ân*ic verses in Arabic with their Dutch translation and arranged around certain themes such as monotheism, unbelief, idolatry and *jihad*. Since most of these were stored in directories referring to Abu Khaled al-Issa, it is plausible that these were used for sessions with him. It seems that he thoroughly familiarized them with the ideas of Sayyid Qutb and Mawdûdî.

The central notion is that God has not only created the universe and humanity, but has also revealed rules for mankind to live by. God, in this perspective, is not only creator and the object of veneration but also lawgiver. Now, monotheism (*tawhîd*) implies that besides God no creator can be recognized and that nothing or no one may be worshipped apart from Him. The novel element is, however, that no human being may legislate, because laying down the law is God's prerogative. States must not enact their own laws but implement the *Shari'a,* God's law. Muslim rulers who refuse to do so commit acts of polytheism (*shirk*) and are, therefore, apostates who deserve the death penalty. A legal system based on man-made laws lacks legitimacy and cannot be recognized. Democracy must therefore be rejected, as, seen from this perspective, it implies slavery and oppression. For it is a political system of domination of men over other men, instead of the domination of God over men. Moreover it is founded on the idea that mankind may create its own laws instead of accepting God's law. Institutions and political and legal systems that violate the principles of monotheism, as well as persons of authority who rule by man-made laws and not according to the *Shari'a,* are called *tâghût,* idols, because they arrogate privileges and positions that belong to God only. Obeying them is denying God His right to be obeyed. Accepting democracy and legal system based on man-mad laws is dubbed *shirk al-hâkimiyya,* i.e., polytheism by recognizing the sovereignty of humans and human institutions, thereby violating God's prerogatives. These ideas deriving from a strict interpretation of the concept of monotheism (*tawhîd*) are perfectly suitable for delegitimizing the political status quo and justify struggle to topple the government.

'Rejecting the Tâghût' (October 2003)

Abu Khaled's lessons were not lost on Bouyeri and he must have been an eager learner. By October 2003 he felt sufficiently confident to produce a text himself entitled *Democratie en Islam* (Democracy and Islam) on the obligation to reject democracy. It is an introduction to the translation of two anonymous English texts that he downloaded from the internet and that argue that democracy is forbidden in Islam and that participating in it by voting or standing for elected bodies is an act of unbelief. In the introduction, addressed to his brethren and sisters, he writes:

> The democratic system is bleeding to death, its putrid face becomes clearer by the day. We live in a world where the supporters of this system set themselves up as the masters of all other inhabitants of the earth. They claim the exclusive right to subject others. The foremost of all democratic countries is the pernicious America, the motherland and model of the democratic system. Although it becomes clearer by the day that democracy is only a smoke curtain to exploit other people as slaves, there

> are still those who cannot free themselves from the intellectual slavery [and think] that this system is indeed the best that has been created for humanity (better that the Shari' a).[3]

In this passage we see that there is an identification of democracy with the West and especially with the United States. This we find in his other writings too. Democracy and 'the West' are often used interchangeably and criticism of Western or American international politics is also addressed to democracy as a political system.

It is evident that Abu Khaled's teachings had borne fruit by then. Bouyeri had been put on track and from the Fall 2003 he continued to develop his ideas himself, aided by the internet. During that Fall and the Spring of 2004 he translated documents gathered from the internet, all of them dealing with the rejection of democratic governments, with the view that resorting to tribunals not based on the Shari' a entails apostasy and with the urgency of establishing a political and legal order based on the Shari' a. A new element is a document on 'loyalty and distance' (Arabic: *al-walâ' wa-l-barâ'a*). This is the principle that Muslims must only consort with and give their loyalty to other Muslims and that they must keep their distance from non-Muslims. Since the definition of who is a Muslim used by these groups is rather narrow, this principle imposes sectarian isolation from mainstream Muslims.

In the introductions to his translations, Bouyeri repeatedly speaks of the struggle between the true Islam and its enemies:

> Since the turning point in our history, better known as 9/11, a struggle like the one between David and Goliath has broken out between the followers of Truth and those of Falsehood. ... We see nowadays that every day the struggle comes closer to us. [Take for instance] the supervised sermons of imams preaching in the service of malicious tyrants. In doing so they give the truth a totally different meaning and show the followers of Truth in a bad light.[4]

'Join the Caravan of Martyrs' (March 2003)

The logical consequence of seeing reality in terms of a struggle between the truth and falsehood was of course a call for participation in that struggle. The first summons to *jihad* dates from March 2003 and is

---
[3] Introduction to *Democratie en islam*, written 13-10-2003.
[4] Kufrdunakufr.doc (22-1-04), introduction to a translated text of Abu Hamza el Masri.

found in a pamphlet entitled 'To catch a wolf.' It is an emotional piece of about 3,000 words written in great anger. Its style is slovenly and it contains passages that are not entirely intelligible. Nevertheless the gist is clear.

The overall message is that Islam is under attack by the West and that this attack must be resisted. The state of the Muslim community is described in almost apocalyptic terms:

> The earth is trembling, the sky is weeping and the wind is raging frenetically. So much injustice, so much misery, so much pain, so many tears, so much Muslim blood being shed daily. It is difficult not to be distressed and dejected when swamped by so many terrible images and reports about our brothers and sisters all over the world.

The sorry state of the Muslim world is in the first place due to Western aggression, aiming at the total destruction of Islam:

> There are dark satanic forces that have sown their seed of evil everywhere in the world. This seed has been sown in the Islamic world in the times of colonialism and has since then taken root. Since the fall of the Ottoman Empire and the Islamic caliphate the enemies of Islam have been active in gradually carrying out their plans aiming at the total destruction of Islam. The Islamic umma, once so powerful and proud, has become no more that a dead drunk and frustrated nation, begging at the doorsteps of the West for a piece of bread. Its honour has no more value than that of a barking mongrel on which passers-by take it out by spitting their gall at it.

The West is not only blamed for defeating the Muslim world but also for the injustice of the unequal distribution of wealth in the world. Addressing the Western leaders, Bouyeri asks rhetorically:

> How did it happen that your bank vaults are full of gold although there are no goldmines in your countries? How did it happen that a rich continent like Africa is poverty-stricken? How did it happen that all those guns, landmines, tanks and other destructive weaponry produced in your democratic countries, have found their way to these poor victims?

However, not only the West carries the blame. Part of the decay is the fault of Muslim leaders who have betrayed their community to its enemies:

> The Islamic *umma* seems to be visited by a cancerous growth that has disseminated all over the body. We are on the edge of an abyss and it seems that it is only a matter of time before we smash ourselves up. We are a frustrated nation betrayed by the so-called leaders of this *umma*, leaders who have sold themselves as cheap whores to the West and allow the spirits and souls of Muslim youth to be poisoned by the poison of *kufr* (unbelief).

The title of the document refers to an Inuit technique to catch wolves: they plant a sharp knife covered with layers of frozen blood in the snow. When a wolf passes he smells the blood, traces the knife and starts licking it, thereby cutting his tongue without noticing it. He then continues to lick his own warm blood and bleeds to death. This is related to a message concerning the nature of democracy: the democratic leaders ('the democratic vampires') try to reduce their subjects to a state of languor and inertia so as to better be able to exploit them. This they do by offering them goodies like coffee shops (where, in the Netherlands, soft drugs can be purchased lawfully), discos, bars and gambling halls, where they become enslaved to their own lusts and desires and lose the will to resist. These goodies are likened to the bloody knife planted in the snow: enjoying them draws the strength from a person and is ultimately fatal.

Bouyeri then seems to suggest that there is a relationship between these goodies, intended to undermine the strength of the people, and the final downfall of the United States, although the passage is not fully clear. It can be read as a message of hope, like the Marxist prophecies of the final downfall of capitalism, but also as an argument for the strength of the elite, whose position is not affected by the ruin of society:

> If we take America, the Mother of all Democracies, as an example and compare the social statistics (crime, violence) with those of other countries then we must conclude that this country is sick to the core. It is only a matter of time before the social order becomes one big chaos. The laughing third parties in this big monopoly game are the democratic vampires. They fortify their bodies by injecting innocent blood into their veins because of their unquenchable thirst for it.

The last message is that a small group of responsible Muslims have emerged in the Netherlands, "because Dutch politics stimulate its citizens (especially the migrants = Muslims) to participate in [discussions on] social questions and to take responsibility." This small group have assumed "social responsibility, not only for the Netherlands but for the whole world and taken upon themselves the task of liberating the world from democratic slavery." Its aim is to establish the domination of Islam and they call on other Muslims to join the *jihad*. In the last paragraph he addresses Muslim youths and shouts (witness the capitalization which is Bouyeri's):

WAKE UP! LOOK AROUND! MUSLIMS ARE BEING SLAUGHTERED AND YOU CANNOT DO ANYTHING BECAUSE YOU ARE BLEEDING TO DEATH. Free yourself! Leave the coffee shop, leave the bar, leave that street corner. Answer the call of LA ILAHA ILLA ALLAH. Join the Caravan of Martyrs. Wake up from your stupor, rise and shake off the dust of humiliation. Rise and answer to the summons for *jihad*.

'… your blood and properties have become halal.' (Summer 2003)

During the Spring of 2004 members of the 'Hofstadgroep' must have discussed what kind of actions they could carry out to help Islam. They may also have talked about violent actions in the Netherlands. However, on this point there existed an ideological problem that had to be resolved. The texts that Bouyeri downloaded from the internet and that inspired him related mainly to the situation in the Islamic world. Even Abu Hamza el-Misri, who was a British citizen and active in London, was hardly concerned with the situation in England, but rather with the Muslim world and could therefore rely on the theories formulated by Qutb and Mawdûdî. Their writings referred to the Muslim world and they argued that Muslim leaders had abandoned true Islam and become apostates. That was their principal justification for a revolutionary struggle against them. This doctrine, however, did not make sense in the Dutch context. Of course, the country was governed by non-Muslims, but not by apostates. And that made an enormous difference.

According to *Shari'a* principle generally accepted among pious Muslim migrants, the relationship of Muslims and the countries where they live, is governed by the notion of a treaty or contract. According to the classical doctrine of the *Shari'a* non-Muslims living in the Dâr al-harb, the Abode of War, i.e., outside the boundaries of the Islamic state and not in a country with which the Islamic state has concluded a treaty, are not protected by the *Shari'a*. The may be killed, enslaved or robbed with impunity. However, if they enter Muslim territory with a pledge of security (*amân*) granted by officials or by any adult male Muslim, their lives, property and freedom are protected by law, on the condition that they respect the laws of the land. Comparable rules apply if a Muslim enters the *Dâr al-Harb* with the express permission of the local non-Muslim authorities. If they grant him protection under the local laws, the Shari`a obligates him to respect these laws. Contemporary Muslims equate visa and residence permits with such a permission and assert that Muslims legally residing in non-Muslim countries are bound by the local laws.

This doctrine posed problems to Bouyeri's ideas of calling for *jihad* in the Netherlands. We have no information on whether this was discussed in the group, but it is likely that it was. They were wont to judge their behaviour by Islamic standards and discuss whether certain acts or ways of dressing were forbidden or permitted. There can be no doubt that lawfulness of the use of violence must have been debated. Two solutions were found as far as we can ascertain from the documents produced during the Summer of 2003. One was the use of violence against individuals, not within the framework of warfare and *jihad*, but by way of punishment for alleged crimes against Islam. The reasoning behind this must have been that in the absence of a really Islamic State and Shari' a courts, true Muslims were entitled or even obliged to punish individuals who committed serious offences. The other solution was to regard the 'treaty' of the Dutch State with Muslim residents as abolished on the ground that the Dutch government had violated it by supporting the U.S. and Israel in their warfare against Islam and by sending troops to Iraq.

There are three translated documents laying the groundwork for violence. They provided justifications and encouragement for violent actions. One text, incidentally the only one directly translated from the Arabic, probably with the help of others, is a *fatwa* by Ibn Taymiyya (d. 1328), stating that it is mandatory to execute persons insulting the Prophet Mohammed. For Ibn Taymiyya this meant that such persons were to be sentenced to death after a trial and a substantiation of the facts. Bouyeri, however, as we know from the ensuing events, misunderstood this and took it as an obligation for individual Muslims to take the law in their own hands. The other document is a recent *fatwa* issued in November 2002 by a certain Hâmid al-`Alî, a radical Muslim scholar from Kuwait, arguing that Yasser Arafat was an apostate because he was in favour of a secularist State in Palestine. The last document is a text listing the blessings of martyrdom and entitled *The battlefield: The safest place on earth*. Its author, Amîr Sulaymân, argues that he participated in *jihad* not because his faith is so strong, but rather because it is weak: death on the battlefield will save him from consequences of his sins and secures for him a privileged position in paradise.

During that Summer Bouyeri produces seven open letters, most of which were published on the internet. Three of them addressed groups of Muslims collectively: a letter to "the mendacious 'ulama' (religious scholars) and imams," summoning them to mend their ways and to convert to true Islam; one addressing Muslim youth and requesting them to set out on a quest for true Islam and the third one depicting in lively terms the torture inflicted by Americans on Iraqi Muslims – reports on the Abu Ghraib prison had been publicized earlier that year – and summoning the entire Muslims *umma* (community) to *jihad* against its enemies. Of the other four, three contained threats against Dutch individuals and one against the Dutch population collectively.

Of the open letters to individuals the most notorious is the one addressing Ayaan Hirsi Ali, at that time a Dutch MP of Somali Muslim origin.[5] Bouyeri had skewered a copy of it to van Gogh's dead body after he had murdered him. Hirsi Ali had become one of the most vociferous critics of Islam in the public debate and had publicly announced that she was no Muslim anymore. The letter is somewhat confused. In the opening paragraphs Bouyeri blames Hirsi Ali not only for apostatizing but also for joining the ranks of the 'soldiers of evil.' On the other hand he alleges that she is an instrument in the hands of a clique of Jewish (and allegedly Jewish) politicians and quotes the *Talmud* 'proving' that non-Jews are not regarded as human and must be killed. These quotations come from an American anti-Semitic pamphlet downloaded by Bouyeri from a fundamentalist Islamic site, which had copied it from an anti-Semitic American site.[6] The letter to Hirsi Ali has a curious end. It does not directly threaten her with death but challenges her to commit suicide. The reasoning behind this is the following: if she really does not believe anymore, she can show in that way that she is not afraid of all horrors that according to the *Qur'ān* are awaiting the unbelievers in the hereafter. Since the letter was found on van Gogh's body it was understood as a death threat against her. On 29 August of that year (actually, after the letter had been written) a short documentary called 'Submission' produced by her and van Gogh had been shown on Dutch

---

[5] On the role of Ayaan Hirsi Ali in the Dutch Islam debate, see Yolanda van Tilborgh, *Wij zijn Nederland: Moslima's over Ayaan Hirsi Ali*. Amsterdam: Van Gennep, 2006; and Rudolph Peters, *A Dangerous Book: Dutch Public Intellectuals and the Qur'ān*. San Domenico di Fiesole, Firenze: European University Institute, Robert Schuman Centre for Advanced Studies, 2006. *EUI Working Papers; RSCAS, 2006/39*. http://www.iue.it/RSCAS/WP-Texts/06_39.pdf

[6] Michael A. Hoffman and Allan R. Critchley, "The Truth about the *Talmud*: A documented exposé of Jewish supremacist hate literature". Http://www.hoffman-info.com/talmudtruth.html (consulted 28-1-2007).

television. This movie was felt by many Dutch Muslims as an outrage against Islam.

Another letter was directed against Ahmed Aboutaleb an Amsterdam alderman of Moroccan descent. He was criticized for being a 'secular Muslim (= *kafir*),' which immediately reminds us of the *fatwa* of Hâmid al-`Alî condemning Arafat for his secular political ideas. The letter concludes with the following warning: "This letter has been drafted in order to warn you and the other millions of the unbelievers for the horrible consequences of their behaviour and to inform you about your status in Islam." Since with status in Islam Bouyeri meant that Aboutaleb was an apostate, the conclusion that this was a threatening letter is fully justified. The last letter to an individual was addressed to the MP Geert Wilders, who is known for his Islamophobic views. Since he uses to dye his hair blond, Bouyeri and his group assumed that he was a homosexual and told him that he should be thrown from the Euro mast, a 185 meter high tower in Rotterdam by way of *Shari'a* punishment.

The last and most threatening letter was the open letter to the Dutch people. In it Bouyeri expounds that a war is going on between the forces of evil, i.e., the coalition led by the United States, and Islam. In this war millions of Muslims have been brutally slaughtered and raped. The Dutch government, the letter goes on, dominated by Zionist Jews, supports Israel in its struggle against Islam and has joined the coalition forces. Since government policy is based on election, the non-Muslims Dutch have become lawful targets: their lives and properties have become *halal*.

> The dark clouds of death assemble over your country. Prepare yourselves for that for which one cannot prepare oneself. The death and torture of our brothers and sisters must be redeemed with your own blood. You have become targets everywhere: in trams, the buses, in trains, in shopping malls etc. It won't take more than a fraction of a second and you'll be in the midst of dead persons. The unbearable stench of death will upset your stomach. You will taste the pain of loss and mutilation. … Life will become Hell for you and you will not find rest until our brothers and sisters have it.

Here ends the process of radicalization of Mohammed Bouyeri. The next thing he did was put his ideas in practice by murdering van Gogh.

Analysis[7]

Although Bouyeri was so far the only Muslim extremist to use violence in the Netherlands, he is not the only young radicalized Dutch Muslim. There are many more, although there is much difference of opinion among their numbers. In this chapter I will briefly discuss the causes of the radicalization process followed by Bouyeri, whereby I will distinguish between personal and social factors. The latter are important in so far as they have an impact on all young Muslims.

Radicalization means protest and resistance against the established order. When young Dutch Muslims radicalize, they criticize and oppose not only the political and social order of the country, but also their own communities and their parents. The radicalization process has two dimensions: on the one hand the rejection of Dutch politics and society and on the other the construction of an Islamic alternative. This is referred to as the search for pure Islam, carried out by having recourse to Islamic fundamentalist ideologies, which do not allow cultural variation and draw strict boundaries between belief and unbelief. This implies a rejection of the forms of Islam of their parents and local mosques, which the radicals regard as being adulterated with local (i.e., Moroccan) cultural elements. In order to show their position and to distance themselves from their communities they often wear distinctive clothes (e.g., for men trousers that leave the ankles free or the Afghan and Pakistani *shalwar* and *qamis* and for women the face veil) and grow a beard.

Although radicalization processes are often chaotic and highly individual, it is nevertheless possible to distinguish three stages in its development: the loss of trust in the political system and social order, the conflict of legitimacy, in which alternatives are developed for the existing political and social order, and finally the crisis of legitimacy, in which the criticism of the political and social orders is extended to their representatives, who are subsequently presented as dehumanized enemies and lawful targets of violent actions.[8] These three stages can be clearly seen in Bouyeri's development. During the first stage he begins to question the Dutch social order and culture and to contrast them with Islamic ideals. The second stage focuses more on politics: the Dutch/Western political system is rejected on Islamic theological grounds

---

[7] The best study about the radicalization of Muslim youths in the Netherlands is Frank Buijs, Froukje Demant, and Atef Hamdy, *Strijders van eigen bodem: Radicale en democratische Moslims in Nederland*. Amsterdam: Amsterdam University Press, 2006.

[8] Buijs et al., *idem.*, p. 17.

and those Muslims who accept it and participate in it are labelled as unbelievers. During the last stage Bouyeri proclaims *jihad* against the Dutch political system, first in a very general way, but later identifying specific persons as lawful objects of attacks. These are either Dutch politicians or Muslim religious leaders. In the end, as we have seen, he threatened to attack citizens indiscriminately.

In publications about Bouyeri, three factors are generally mentioned that in combination have triggered his radicalization. These are highly individual ones, and may lead to radicalization in some but not in others. The first one is that he served a prison sentence of several weeks in Summer 2001. During his time in prison he started to study the *Qur'ân*. The second factor is his mother's death by the end of that year. This may have caused some emotional instability. He himself said later that with his mother's death he started a quest for the truth. The last factor is the refusal of the local administration (May 2002) and the Ministry of Social Affairs (December 2002) to support and fund his plans for a centre for Moroccan youths in the neighbourhood where he lived. Whereas the first factors contributed to a reinforcement of his Islamic identity, the last one made him loose his trust in Dutch politics.

These individual factors are important for explaining Bouyeri's ideas and actions. The social factors, however, are significant for explaining the upsurge of Muslim radicalism in the Netherlands. In her book on religious terrorism,[9] Jessica Stern argues that its most important causes are alienation and humiliation (together with territorial conflicts). Sentiments of alienation and humiliation are widespread among young Muslims, especially among those of Moroccan descent. Alienation, the feeling that one is not a part of Dutch society and is separate from it because of hostility, is the result of isolation and exclusion. Due to high unemployment rates, lack of school success, housing in migrant neighbourhoods and discrimination, many young Muslims become isolated from Dutch society and feel that they are excluded. Such feelings may be exacerbated if the public discourse is hostile to Islam and the culture of migrants. In the early periods of migration culture did not play an important role in the public debate. It focussed on the social and economic factors that hindered the integration of migrants and on the means to eliminate these. However, during the 1990s cultural issues became more prominent in politics and the public debate. This implied a change in perspective: whereas previously it was assumed

---

[9] Jessica Stern, *Terror in the Name of God: Why Religious Militants Kill*. New York: Harper Collins, 2003.

that the government and society at large should remove the obstacles blocking integration, now differences in culture were presented as the main impediment. And the answer was that the integration of migrants could only be achieved by cultural assimilation. In other words, the blame as laid on the migrants themselves. At the same time their culture was narrowed down to their religion. Almost all problems and frictions connected with migration were now attributed to Islam. As a result, the migration and integration debate became an Islam debate in which voices that were critical of Islam and often Islamophobic were the loudest. This affected especially well-educated young Muslim migrants. For some of them this resulted in feelings of humiliation.

In Bouyeri's writings both sentiments can be traced: alienation from Dutch society and politics made him reject democracy and, in the end, call for indiscriminate violence against the whole population in order to establish an Islamic state with a sharia's legal system, as an alternative. Humiliation led him to the legitimization of the killing of prominent critics of Islam such as Ayaan Hirsi Ali and the MP Geert Wilders.

Conclusions

Since the murder of the Dutch film maker Theo van Gogh, more terrorist assaults have been committed in Europe: the train bombing in Madrid and the underground bombings in London. It is striking, however, that there seem to be enormous differences between the groups responsible for these assaults on the one hand and Bouyeri and his group on the other. Bouyeri and his group had a very specific profile. The main difference is that the Spanish and English groups had intensive contacts with organisations in the Islamic world, whereas Bouyeri c.s. did not. During the police investigations and the trials no evidence was found for international contacts, with the exception of the role of the Syrian preacher. The perpetrators in Spain and England, on the other hand, appear to have had intensive contacts with Morocco and Pakistan respectively. The Dutch group, therefore, is a clear example of home-grown terrorism. Their main source for their interpretation of Islam was the internet. Bouyeri translated documents he found there and wrote his own treatises and open letters. These must have served as texts for ideological schooling of the group. The presence of this body of material is a second reason why this group is special. For it allows us to follow closely their trajectory of radicalization.

ISLAM AND EUROPE IN THE AGE OF INTERCIVILIZATIONAL CONFLICT DIVERSITY AND THE CHALLENGES

Bassam Tibi

The deliberations and the entire reasoning undertaken in this lecture are based on two major assumptions. The first of which refers to the increasing significance of Islam in the new century, not only for the world at large[1] but also and in particular for Europe.[2]

The new place of Islam being the object of the first assumption relates to the double process of religionization of politics (the return of the sacred in a global garb) and of the politicization of religion. At issue are interrelated processes that touch on Europe on the following two levels:

---

[1] * This chapter includes a radically rewritten text of the free-speech lecture delivered at the Leysen Forum in Louvain. The text was transformed from spoken to written language and footnoted. With regard to the character of the lecture as an overview of my research and thinking about Islam and Europe in the past 30 years I hope for the indulgence of the reader that the footnoting exceeds in its references to my work allowed standards. After all I am the founder of Euro-Islam and Islamology, as a study of Islam and conflict. I acknowledge my gratitude to Prof. Marie-Claire Foblets, whom I first met at the University of California/Berkeley in 1994 and after a break of almost one and half a decade again in Louvain at her invitation to deliver this prestigious Leysen-Forum-Lecture.

The political theorist John Brenkman, *The Contradiction of Democracy. Political Theory after 9/11* (Princeton/NY: Princeton University Press, 2007) contends in the introduction to his book on p. 21 that "Islam ... is broiled in a geopolitical civil world" that also affects Europe and later adds on p. 165 the "unfortunate truth: ... most of the dangers are coming from the Muslim world. The US and Europe must learn how to deal with the seemingly endless conflicts". Similarly one reads in the issue of *The Economist* of November 2007 with the cover story "The New Wars of Religion" and special report "On Faith and Politics. About the New Place of Religion in International Conflict and War" that Islam is pivotal for post-bipolar conflict. Then, *The Economist* suggests : ".... The White House might be going to hell (or at least to H. Clinton), but Europe faces a worse nightmare: a combined descent into Godlessness, and then a takeover by Islam". *The Economist* of November 3-9, 2007, special report, p. 8. See also the reference in note 14 and the part on Europe in the book referenced in the ensuing note 2.

[2] For more details: B. Tibi, *Political Islam, World Politics and Europe. Democratic Peace and Euro-Islam vs. Global Jihad* (New York: Routledge, 2008), Part III.

1. Islam constitutes a part of the European international environment and is therefore ranked by the EU as the neighbourhood of Europe[3] (the transnational level)
2. Islam creates a Diaspora of 20 millions within Europe(the inner European level in an age of global migration) with a potential of an Islamization of Europe[4] a theme treated as taboo and therefore is silenced.

The second assumption relates to the new concept that cultural tensions lead to conflict[5] and they indeed do so. Islam is viewed as a cultural system[6] that, if politicized, develops to a source of an inter-civilizational conflict.[7] The politization of a cultural system results in religious fundamentalism. This phenomenon occurs in all religions and is not specific to Islam. In the case of Islam religion is, however, based on a universalism that underpins the development of local conflicts to international ones. The distinction between Islam as a faith/ethics, and Islamism as a totalitarian ideology[8] of – a religious fundamentalism[9] is most important. It contributes to protecting the analysis of religious-cultural tensions and of their development to a conflict from the well-known accusation of Islamophobia. To be sure, in some few cases this reproach has a point and is justified. Only in these cases, the involved

---

[3] Michael Emersson, ed., *Democratization in the European Neighbourhood* (Brussels: CEPS, 2005), herein the chapter on Islam by B. Tibi, pp. 93-116.

[4] M. Castells and N. AlSayyad, eds, *Muslim Europe or Euro-Islam* (London and Berkeley: Lexington Books, 2002), herein the chapter on Euro-Islam by B. Tibi, pp. 31-52.

[5] On this concept see the volume edited by Helmut Anheier and Y. Raj Isar, *Conflict and Tensions* (New York: Sage, 2007). It is based on "The Globalization and World Cultures Research Project". The volume includes B. Tibi, "Islam between Religious-Cultural Practice and Identity Politics", pp. 221-23

[6] Clifford Geertz views religion as a cultural system in his collection of essays: *The Interpretation of Culture* (New York: Basic Books, 1973), pp. 87-125. For an application of this concept to Islam see B. Tibi, *Islam between Culture and Politics* (New York: Palgrave, 2001), updated and heavily expanded edition 2005, Chapter One, pp. 28-52.

[7] At the research project on this issue chaired by Shahram Akbarzadeh and Fethi Mansouri, the concept of intercivilizational conflict was presented in the paper by B. Tibi, "*Jihad*ism and the Intercivilizational Conflict", which was published as Chapter 4 in the volume edited by the chairpersons of the project: *Islam and Political Violence. Muslim Diaspora and Radicalism in the West* (London: Taures, 2007), pp. 39-64.

[8] On this distinction see Peter Demant, *Islam vs. Islamism* (Westport/Connecticut: Praeger, 2006) and B. Tibi, "Between Islam and Islamism", in Tami A. Jacoby and Brent Sasley, eds, *Redefining Security in the Middle East* (Manchester University Press, 2002), p. 62-82.

[9] B. Tibi, *The Challenge of Fundamentalism. Political Islam and the New World Disorder* (Berkeley: University of California Press, 1998, updated edition 2002).

bias have to be taken seriously. However, the general accusation of an Islamophobia accusation has also become a convenient instrument in the hands of Islamists. They use this accusation not only to prevent, or even incriminate any criticism of their totalitarian political activities, but also to delegitimate real fears related to their *jihad*ist terrorism.

The two outlined assumptions point at a crisis-ridden situation that emerges from a conflict on the two levels mentioned, i.e., within Europe (Islam Diaspora) and at Europe's international borders (Islam is neighbourhood) in the Southern Mediterranean. Therefore, a further assumption has to be added.

The third assumption is that new patterns of conflict resolution are needed. These three assumptions guide the reasoning of this lecture. Therefore, one of the issue areas addressed in this lecture is the intercivilizational dialogue. It is viewed as a means for peaceful conflict resolution. The dialogue between Europe and the world of Islam referred to in the meaning of a peaceful conflict resolution is not a rhetoric and it has substance that makes it different from the established dialogue and its mostly dishonest practices. The established channels of the industry of a self-gratifying Christian-Islam dialogue offer a 'first-class ticket to nowhere', to use the American expression for trash. This kind of dialogue is identified as dishonest, because it is based on an evasion of all pending issues, above all the hot-bottom issues of conflict. Therefore, it is made clear at the very outset that I dissociate my reasoning not only from all kinds of 'clash', but also from a dishonest rhetorical dialogue of the so-called 'alliance of civlizations'. To be sure, a conflict is not a clash and it is possible to prevent the clash of civilizations[10] through a peaceful conflict resolution.

Introduction

Guided by the three assumptions made, the issue focussed on in the present analysis relates to the historical and the contemporary relations between Europe and the world of Islam. When it comes to the present, then the lecture is guided by the spirit of an enlightened form of Euro-Islam. I acknowledge my awareness of the fact that I am pretty much a lone voice in this venture and that the point of departure of

---

[10] See the volume of the former President of Germany, Roman Herzog, ed., *Preventing the Clash of Civilizations* (New York: St. Martin's Press, 1999), also co-authored by B. Tibi, "International Morality and Cross-Cultural Bridging", pp. 107-126.

the following reasoning is not a popular one. I commence with the idea that the dialogue in Europe between the *newcomers*, the Muslim immigrants, and the Europeans has to deal with the way of how each party conceives values. In this context I state a conflict (see note 7). It is exactly this fact on the ground that is deliberately ignored and that is why it is not a popular approach in Europe to address this matter in a conflict analysis.

In this introduction the significance of culture and civilization is emphasized, because both matter to the analysis of the conflict to be analyzed. Since the 1990s it has become clear that cultures and religions affect post-bipolar politics. This is not an invention of Samuel Huntington, but it was his accomplishment to bring the issue to the fore and to launch a heated debate on it. Despite the fact that my book on this issue was published ahead a year prior to the one by Huntington,[11] I failed to unleash this debate. I engaged in writing that book back in 1994 at the University of California/Berkeley as a visiting faculty where I first met my Louvain host, Prof. Marie-Claire Foblets; she knows of the link to Huntington and of his phone calls to me at Berkeley. In fact, Huntington and myself are in disagreement on basic issues, but I nevertheless refuse to join the demonization of his person and of his work, as it happens particularly not only in Europe, but also in the United States. Recently, some friends of Samuel Huntington had to publish an announcement in the *New York Times*, while acting as *liberal* Americans to state 'our colleague Samuel Huntington is not a racist'. Huntington might be wrong on a count of issues, but he neither is a Cold War ideologue, nor a racist, as some contend. It is a kind of a demonization of a Harvard scholar, when these invectives are instigated. In this furious and deplorable kind of debate the distinction between the notion of critique and propaganda is fully lost. Also in the West, as in the world of Islam, particularly in the Middle-East it has become difficult in recent times to engage in a real criticism and not to comply with the censorship of political correctness.

A prominent and courageous Muslim and lecturer in this series, Sadiq Jalal al-Azm, although he is quite offensive in turning the tables around on foes, he is pertinent for the context of these deliberations. He

---

[11] Samuel Huntington, *Clash of Civilizations* (New York: Simon & Schuster, 1996) and a year ahead B. Tibi, *Krieg der Zivilisationen* (Hamburg: Hoffmann & Campe, 1995). In a personal letter to me of March 30, 1995, Huntington acknowledged thankfully receiving this book and expressed his appreciation in this phrase, "skimming through the book, I could see that you developed very powerful arguments on the role of civilization". Unfortunately, Huntington declined to cite my book in his own.

criticized the thinking of Edward Said and his formula of 'Orientalism' in ridiculing it as an 'Orientalism in reverse'. I refer to this Muslim thinker, because his thoughts support the thoughts unfolded in the present lecture.

Back in 1968 al-Azm published an important book in Arabic under the title *Self-criticism after the Defeat*.[12] The title relates to the Six-Days-War, when twenty-two Arab states were defeated; they lost a war against the tiny state of Israel. How could that happen? Sadiq Jalal al-Azm asked that question and challenged Arab Muslims to learn a criticism of the self. Criticism is equated in Arabic with 'disparagement/*hija*". Therefore, the need to reiterate that the idea of an intercivilizational conflict and the critique of totalitarian Islamism are two different issues; they have nothing to do with an alleged or real Islamophobia and this hint is the justification of the reference to the thinking of Sadiq al-Azm.

In this lecture the major themes are those of culture related to Europe and diversity in an age of global migration. In a first step I shall deal with Europe and diversity to move then in a second step to an effort at underpinning the argument of an interaction between two parties. This implies the need to acquire knowledge about the other. The third part of this venture is about the limits of cultural difference. I view diversity as enriching, but acknowledge some limits to it. Therefore, the issue is addressed in the context of diversity and pluralism. The lecture concludes in talking about the policy implications and the measures needed for dealing with the pending conflict.

Europe and Diversity

When one talks about diversity, one has to acknowledge that we are all as humans entitled to rights based on sharing the same dignity. However, humans are culturally different species. There's nothing wrong with this statement as well as the one of conflict that arises from tensions related to difference (see note 5). These conflicts could result in bloodletting as this happens in many places in the world, most recently in Iraq. And this might happen in Europe as well. There is no exclusion. I am aware of the fact that Europeans do not like to hear this message and the related alert. The increasing diversity in Europe brings with

---

[12] Sadiq J. al-Azm, *al-Naqd al-dhati ba'd al-hazimah* (Self-Criticism after the Defeat) (Beirut: al-Tali'a, 1968).

it a conflict and the Europeans need to open their mind for scenarios related to the new realities for dealing with this potential of conflict. If one talks about diversity and relates it to conflict one takes the risk in Europe of becoming a *persona non grata*. This is my repeated personal experience.

In a project conducted at the UC Berkeley on *Islam and the Changing Identity of Europe* a group of scholars engaged in thinking about Europe and diversity (see note 4), it was acknowledged that most European societies, which view themselves as quite homogenous and therefore lack an experience of dealing with diversity are currently changing through migration. Since the late twentieth century, in particular since the end of the Cold War, Europe has become a major attraction for and a recipient of a global migration. In terms of statistics and in comparison to its populace of more than 400 million Western Europe of today is receiving more migrants than the classical country of migration, the United States of America. This is an undeniable scientific fact, which Europeans are culturally and ethnically not yet in a position to come to grips with. They continue to view the incoming peoples as aliens and fail to be inclusive in giving them a European identity related to a sense of belonging to Europe as a new home. To be sure, in order to become a European citizen of the heart is not only the homework of immigrants, it is also a homework for Europeans themselves.[13]

Despite the claim to be a civic nation it is a fact that Europe has become a major place for global migration were Europeans continue to think and to behave in an ethnic manner (see note 16). Of course, there has been a positive change in a transition from earlier Eurocentric sentiments to a new kind of cultural opening. However when one looks at this change in more details, there will be an disillusionment. The problem is contemporary nihilism spreading as a cultural relativism of self-denial among European intellectuals. To be sure, this is not what Europe needs to meet the challenge of cultural open-mindedness under conditions of an increasing diversity.

There are two developments in contemporary Europe that contradict one another. First, Europeans are moving from the extreme of Eurocentrism to the other extreme of civilizational self-denial. This is exactly what most contemporary European intellectuals do. They engage in denying themselves and Europe a civilizatonial identity. In a book on this subject, I describe this process in more details and state

---

[13] B. Tibi, A Migration Story. From Muslim Immigrants to Citizens of the Heart?, in *The Fletcher Forum of World Affairs* vol. 31, 1(2007), pp. 147-168.

a transition from the evil of Euro-centrism to the other of nihilism.[14] This development is contradicted by another trend to more exclusive ethnicity in Europe, to be addressed later on.

In this context, I refer to the last great philosopher in Islam, Ibn Khaldun, whom I admire without any limitation. Ibn Khaldun (died 1406) outlined in his work a philosophy of history based on the concept of '*Asabiyya*'.[15] This term can be translated with Montesquieu's 'esprit de corps' meaning the 'self-awareness' of a civilisation. The birth of a civilization starts with a strong *Asabiyya* and it declines when this *Asabiyya* weakens. For Ibn Khaldun a weak awareness of the self is an indication of civilizational decay; it is not to be confused with open-mindedness. Ibn Khaldun was commemorated in 2006 in Spain, 600 years after his death. At this European commemoration of Ibn Khaldun I had the honor to give in Granada a keynote address in which I asked: What is the state of a European *Asabiyya* under conditions of global migration and increasing diversity? The answer is not a pleasant one.

Europe and its Civilizational Identity in its Interaction with Islam

With a further reference to the increasing diversity within Europe I fail to see a positive accommodation of the change. The move from the extreme of Euro-centrism to the other extreme of self-denial among European intellectuals is not a positive sign. Common Europeans respond to the process of self-ethnicization of migrant communities with a European self-ethnicization. Within the framework of identity politics two patterns of ethnicity reinforce one another.[16] In this context, ethnicity revolves around identity politics based on the politicization of difference which makes it difficult to accommodate it in a conflict situation.

---

[14] B. Tibi, *Europa ohne Identität?* (Munich: Bertelsmann, 1998). A Dutch edition was published under the title *Europa zonder identiteit? De crisis van de multiculturele samenleving* (Oosterhout, Belgium: Deltas, 2000).

[15] On Ibn Khaldun, *Muqaddima* and his philosophy see the major monograph by Muhsen Mahdi, *Ibn Khaldun's Philosophy of History* (London: Allen and Unwin, 1957) and the Ibn-Khaldun-chapter 6 in: B. Tibi, *Der wahre Imam* (Munich: Piper, 1996), pp. 179-209.

[16] In a symposium at Stanford University's Humanities Center on "Ethnicity in Today's Europe" in November 2007 I presented one year after this Leysen-Forum-Lecture at Louvain a research paper in which these ethnicization processes in Europe are stated and analyzed in full details. A publication is forthcoming.

Fashionable multiculturalism is mostly positive about the migrant communities engaging in identity politics, but not about the same process in one's own society. Simultaneously a very weak self-awareness of Europeans coincides with the ethnic identity politics of particular communities within the migrant Diaspora. In this situation, the balance is missing and a true dialogue is needed. As earlier stated, Christian-Islamic dialogue is not a proper model for a dialogue between the civilizations. It is self-evident that dialogue presupposes a clear identity of the parties involved. In the UC Berkeley project, conducted by the Centre for European Studies and the Centre for Middle-Eastern Studies of that university between 1998-2002 the assumption of a changing identity of Europe was made and it was related to Islamic migration (note 4). What is the civilizational identity of Europe and in what conflict is it involved in the context of the change mentioned? There are two options and, again many Europeans do not like to listen to this message. The options are expressed in the title of the book based on the UC Berkeley project: Euro-Islam or Muslim Europe? That reasoning was continued in the new century at Cornell University in a project on *Religion in an Expanding Europe* at which the alternatives were presented in this phrasing: Europeanizing Islam or the Islamization of Europe.[17]

The interrelation of religion and politics in Europe is not well understood by Europeans, nor that when politics are articulated in a religious language the outcome is a religious fundamentalism. This phenomenon occurs in all religions throughout the world, but Europe is an exception. The Fundamentalism Project at the American Academy of Arts and Sciences[18] supports this statement. The project's director, Professor Martin Marty, once stated: "Europe is a white empty paper on the geopolitical map of fundamentalism". In fact, religion – as *The Economist* notes (see note 1) – is declining in Europe, where people not only don't go to church and barely have a religious identity, but also have great difficulties to understand how immigrants bring back religion and its meaning to the Old World. The German Jewish scholar Michael Wolffsohn complained in a 2006-*Frankfurter Allgemeine Zeitung* article about the German *Religionsanalphabeten* (religion illiterates). Other

---

[17] See Peter Katzenstein and T. Byrnes, eds, *Religion in an Expanding Europe* (New York: Cambridge University Press, 2006). The volumes includes as a chapter 8: B. Tibi, "Europeanizing Islam or the Islamization of Europe. Political Democracy vs. Cultural Difference" (New York: Cambridge University Press, 2006), pp. 204-224.

[18] Martin Marty and Scott Appleby, eds, *The Fundamentalism Project*, 5 vols, published by Chicago University Press between 1990 and 1995. Vol. 2 includes my contribution on the worldview of Sunni Arab Islamic fundamentalists as Chapter 4, pp. 73-224.

Europeans share this feature and do not understand this phenomenon and respectively not the Islamic challenge.[19]

The intermingling of religion, politics and society in the twenty-first century is not an academic question. If Europeans continue to fail to integrate the now twenty million Muslims living in Europe – more will come and then the number shall double and triple – then the dream of some leaders of the Muslim community, a dream of Muslim Europe, will become within the reach. Does Europe have a civilizational identity? The prominent Princeton professor Bernard Lewis was asked in an interview with the German newspaper *Die Welt*, "*Europa wird islamisch* (Europe will become Islamic)", about the future of Europe in the twenty-first century. He predicted in his response a Muslim Europe in the foreseeable future. I contradicted him as a Muslim living in Europe who wants to be a European in stating, the problem is not the number of Muslim people living in Europe, but rather what Islam is coming to Europe. Is it European Islam, enlightened Islam compatible and consonant with the civilizational identity of Europe, or is it *Shari'a*-Islam? This is the real issue and this is what the future of Europe is all about. It is noteworthy that no comment came from the European side. The debate was published in Germany, but covered by a bulletin read by American senators and other US opinion leaders, namely in the *Standard Weekly* of Washington.[20] My comment is in a value-free language with a reference to the philosophy of Ibn Khaldun: the state of the European *Asabiyya* is weak.

Cultural Difference and the Challenge of Religion: The Limits

Neo-absolutism and Cultural Relativism in Europe

There is a simultaneity of Europeans with weak *Asabiyya* who equate open-mindedness with cultural relativism and other people who stand to their values with a sentiment of a neo-absolutism. In this context cultural relativists enter new conflicts over values and are in general unprepared for this. The conflict between the Islamist *Shari'a*-based neo-absolutism

---

[19] B. Tibi, *Die islamische Herausforderung. Religion und Politik im Europa des 21. Jahrhunderts* (Darmstadt: Primus, 2007).

[20] The report was published in *The Standard Weekly*/Washington DC of October 4, 2004 by Christopher Caldwell, "Islamic Europe?", pp. 15-16.

and cultural relativism ends with no compromise, but rather with a submission of the relativist to the neo-absolutist claims; they do this in the name of a questionable multicultural, i.e. indiscriminate tolerance. Nihilist cultural relativism and religious neo-absolutism are the wrong response to the challenge of cultural diversity, but nevertheless are in alliance as strange bedfellows.

I maintain that European societies are – despite the claim to be a civic nation – basically ethnic. There is confusion among Europeans between homogeneity and ethnic exclusiveness. I have lived for forty-five years in Germany and have never succeeded to be accepted as a German, despite my German citizenship, the only one I have. In legal terms, I am this German citizen, but there is nothing beyond that: My earlier conception of the self that "I'm a German" by values and culture proved, however, to be an illusion, because the German nation is not based on a civic culture, but rather on ethnicity. It is not a contradiction in Germany to say "Tibi is a Syrian, who holds a German passport". In America you are American in all terms when you acquire US citizenship. What can be done to avert the catastrophe Europe is heading to? The alert of the Intifada of the banlieues of October/November 2005 was not well-taken. Will this become a model?

There is an alternative: From the standpoint of this lecture cultural pluralism integrated into the concept of European Islam promises to be the better alternative. There are great obstacles in the pursuit of this alternative. At first there are those among Europeans who engage in obstruction. Then there are those among the Muslim Diaspora who undermine integration.

Ethnic exclusiveness among European peoples is one of the greatest obstacles for a proper dealing with cultural difference. In response to this obstacle one encounters another one on the Muslim side, namely self-ethnicization. Europeans and Muslim immigrants are two parties who fail to understand one another. This situation is exacerbated by a third obstacle: the social marginalization. In France you have the *banlieues de l'Islam*, the suburbs of Paris, described by Gilles Kepel in one of his books that carries this formula in its title,[21] on the one hand, and the self-congratulatory civic French, who are truly ethnic, on the other.

In a Diaspora situation one faces cultural attitudes based on neo-absolutism nurtured by a socio-economic marginalization. One cannot understand this combination in a reductionist manner. In the process

---

[21] Gilles Kepel, *Les banlieues de l'islam* (Paris: Gallimard, 1987).

of a religionization of politics one finds an interplay between religion and politics in society. None of the pending problems can be reduced to a social or economic situation. Europeans seem to have only little knowledge about the issue, which explains the lack of a useful policy for dealing with great diversity in Europe. In this situation the first prudent thing to do is to admit a free debate on these issues.

Integration vs. Islamic Enclaves

The poor conditions of a European *Asabiyya* combined with the nihilism of cultural relativism contribute to the lack of integration of Muslim immigrants. Only societies with a strong civilizational identity could be inclusive in the sense of offering to newcomers a shared identity. The mushrooming of parallel societies named Islamic enclaves existing in Europe but are not part of it, was mentioned by John Kelsey.[22] This is not diversity, but rather fragmentation. In a society people are different and there is nothing wrong with that because difference can be a source of inspiration and there is a democratic right to it. However, the fragmentation of society is detrimental, it is something other than just difference. When it comes to cultural difference then it has to be combined with pluralism. Diversity is precious, but diversity has to be established within pluralism, it cannot be accommodated by relativism nor by absolutism.

In short, European ethnicity paired with the spread of the totalitarian ideology of Islamism in the Islam Diaspora in Europe as well as with the self-ethnicization of the immigrants are the background of the failure to integrate Muslim immigrants to citizens of the heart (see note 13). Europe not only needs solutions, but also an awareness of this need. It is not in place and if this does not change, then there can be no light at the end of the tunnel.

What are the Limits of Diversity?

Every society has a civilizational identity. An open society is expected to be inclusive, however, the inclusion has to be in harmony with this identity and to be bound to a set of values. Karl Popper establishes his

---

[22] John Kelsey; *Islam and War* (Louisville: J. Fox Press, 1993) speaks of "Islamic communities (as) a sort of sectarian enclaves ... in the West, but not of it", p. 118.

model of an open society on tolerance, but he maintains that tolerance has its limits: intolerance cannot be admitted in the name of tolerance.[23] I learned the idea of Europe from my Jewish professor Max Horkheimer, who established the Frankfurt School during the early decades of the twentieth century.[24] In 1933 he had to flee Germany in order to survive the Holocaust. However, Horkheimer returned to Germany from US exile, because he loved the idea of Europe. In his preface to the two volumes *Kritische Theorie*,[25] – considered to be his legacy – he writes his will: Europe has to be protected as *Insel in einem Ozean der Gewaltherrschaft* (island of freedom in an ocean of violent rule) 'against any totalitarianism'. He mentions two: Nazism and Stalinism. In my book on Europe (see note 14) dedicated to the memory of Horkheimer I add the new totalitarianism: Islamism and place it in defense of Europe on the list of totalitarianisms and enemies of the open society. Euro-Islam is the alternative to Islamism. During the Dutch presidency of the European Union I presented in English a paper on Euro-Islam as an alternative and it was published in Dutch by *Nexus*.[26]

In short, there are limits to diversity. Totalitarian as much as pre-modern attitudes and views cannot be admitted in the name of diversity. If somebody says "we want to establish *Shari'a* in Europe" and asks for this claim a multicultural tolerance, then the proper response should be: "no *Shari'a* in Europe". This response does not contradict my firm standing for diversity. Practices of pre-modern cultures, which include genital violence (circumcision), persecuting the unbelievers, beating women, gender inequality etc. cannot be accepted in the name of diversity. Also the political views are to be rejected, if they are not consonant with democracy, and or even totalitarian. The concept of '*Hakimiyyat Allah* (God's rule)', which is the core idea of Islamism has to be denied admission and one cannot let it go in the name of diversity.

Religious tolerance is precious, but it cannot be extended to political Islam, which reinvents many of the concepts in Islam and makes out of Islam an Islamism. Political Islam is a totalitarian ideology against the open society.[27]

---

[23] Karl Popper, *The Open Society and its Enemies*, 2 vols (London: Routledge, 1945).
[24] Martin Jay, *The Dialectical Imagination. A History of The Frankfurt School* (Boston: Little and Brown, 1973).
[25] Max Horkheimer, *Kritische Theorie*, 2 vols (Frankfurt: S. Fischer, 1968), in particular preface p. XIII to vol. I.
[26] B. Tibi, "Euro-islam. Juridisch burgerschap en burgers van het hart", in *Nexus*, issue 41/2005, pp. 173-203.
[27] B. Tibi, *Political Islam*, referenced in note 2.

Conclusions and Policy Recommendations: Europe and Islam

In the US part of my academic life since 1982 (Harvard), and in particular since I joined the Fundamentalism Project of The American Academy of Arts and Sciences I learned to combine social-scientific analysis with policy recommendation. Unlike in Germany, in the US it is expected from a social science professor who engages in research, for instance about a conflict not only to analyze and to explain, but also to have an answer to the question: what is to do? This issue would be related to the policy implications of an analysis.

In applying this approach to this Leysen Forum Lecture I refer to the late M.I.T. professor Myron Weiner, who descended from a Jewish migrant family from the Baltic. Weiner wrote a major book on *The Global Migration Crisis*[28] before he passed away; he was the first scholar who related migration to conflict and security. The cited book includes a full chapter on migration and security. Some people would see in this analysis a kind of a xenophobia, and accuse of a panicking. To be sure, immigrants not only bring their manpower, but also the conflicts existing in their countries of origin as well. For example the Kurds in Germany make the Turkish-Kurdish conflict a European one through migration: Muslim immigrants bring the problems of the world of Islam to Europe, and Islamism as well as its networks are the toughest among them. Europe is the core for these networks. Within these channels Islamism comes to Europe to the extent of making Europe, as Francis Fukuyama contends, "a battlefront of Islamism". It uses identity politics in this pursuit for the promotion of its concerns.

In line with the research completed by Myron Weiner I address the issue and ask how to deal with it. Integration seems to be the best policy approach. It is a fact that al-Qaeda is now present throughout Europe and also Islamism in general. During the Lebanon war of 2006 one German politician was asked by *The New York Times*: "What is your standing about this?" His answer was: "We have to be careful and calm, we cannot act freely due to the fact that we shelter nine hundred organized Hezbollah people in Germany in addition to three hundred Hamas partisans". The German politician was concerned that these Islamists could be provoked by an action of the German state. There is a serious security problem. I cannot offer you all the needed recipes here, but think a politics of integration is the best avenue to make

---

[28] Myron Wiener, *The Global Migration Crisis* (New York: Harper Collins Publ., 1995).

Muslims European citizens of heart, i.e. people who embrace the idea of Europe, love Europe, and who identify with it. If this task can be done successfully, then one can dissociate Muslim immigrants from the Islamists and from the *jihad*ists (see note 13).

In an early book written in the aftermath of 9/11 *Islamische Zuwanderung* (2002) and in a recent one of 2007 concepts for the future of Europe are introduced to protect political democracy while acknowledging cultural difference. However, the challenge to democracy in the name of difference and in the name of diversity should not be accepted. Islamists come to Europe, abuse democracy in the pursuit of their totalitarian agenda, but Europe has no proper response. There is a pertinent story. The one of Copenhagen in December 2006. By then and in the shadow of the conflict over the Mohammed cartoons 'The Muslim Association of Democrats in Denmark' was established by Danish Muslims to counter by then the Palestinian Imam Abu-Laban, who orchestrated the conflict. The late Abu-Laban also guided one of the leading mosques of Copenhagen and incited hatred there. The Muslim-democratic message to Abu-Laban, who later passed away, was: "You claim to speak in the name of Islam, but we are Muslims too, and speak as pro-democracy Muslims, and challenge you. You do not represent us" This is an example for political democracy above cultural difference and in respect for Europe. I was invited by these Muslim democrats to present the concept of Euro-Islam. This concept is a policy recommendation. What is it all about?

In 1982 I visited for the first time in my life an Islamic country, which is not an Arab one. It was Senegal. There in West Africa I observed Muslim cultural practices alien to me as an Arab Muslim, who grew up in Damascus. Every time I said "mais, ce n'est pas islamique!". I was given the answer by my African hosts: "mais c'est africain"!! This is the background of the concept of Euro-Islam presented as a policy recommendation. For your understanding I should provide you with some historical facts: Islam came to Senegal from the North, from Morocco, between the 13th and the 15th century. Today, Islam prevails in West Africa as a local culture that combines Islam and Africa in an Afro-Islam. Senegalese are Muslims, but their Islamic identity is deeply rooted in Africa. Some pre-Islamic practices were fully integrated. Their Islam is not alien to Africa, but the Islam of Muslim immigrants is alien to Europe. This is a fact. 1992, ten years after, I was invited by a French institution to join the deliberation about an integration to replace the earlier French concept of assimilation. Prior to this effort, the French were committed to the concept of assimilation: if you want to be French, then you have to assimilate: *être français est assimiler*. This concept worked sometimes, but since the late '80s and in particular early '90s it proved not feasible. To replace the concept of assimilation with the one of integration one has to limit the scope of inclusion into society to the acceptance of civic values of the French revolution, above all: the concept of 'laïcité'. When it comes to Islam one has to add 's', i.e., 'Islams' to put in plural. Can there be a European Islam (Euro-Islam) as a variety?

In my 1992-Paris paper *Les conditions de l'islam*[29] I employed my Senegalese experience, where Islam is African and asked along the Africanization of Islam there the question about Europeanizing Islam, of course only in Europe. This is the policy I recommend ever since 1992. I have been working on this concept for two decades and view it as a ground for the needed solutions for the issue. Euro-Islam is an alternative to nihilist multiculturalism, and also to Islamism. I propose to adopt cultural pluralism to replace multiculturalism. Euro-Islam could be integrated into a cultural pluralism, while multiculturalism allows Muslim enclaves of religious communities as parallel societies and thus results in fragmentation of society. In all frankness: This would be the end of Europe.

I conclude this lecture in stating that Muslims and Europeans need to live together in Europe in peace and freedom. The open society is the framework to do so, both need to share a consensus over basic civic values. We Muslims are educated to look at ourselves as superior to others: *Siyadat al-Islam*. This should not be confused with modern fundamentalism, for the concept is much older. We have to learn that this attitude of Muslims in Europe is unacceptable. If one considers the self superior to others then no diversity can thrive in pluralism. The acceptance of diversity has therefore to be limited. On the ground of establishing a commonality of shared values of civility, of civil society, of democracy and individual human rights, diversity in the outlined understanding of pluralism could be the avenue for Europe in the twenty-

---

[29] The first introduction of the concept of Euro-Islam took place in Paris 1992 (see the report of *Frankfurter Allgemeine Zeitung* of December 1992, p. 14, published under the title: "Euro-Islam or Ghetto-Islam". The paper itself, "Les conditions d'un euro-islam", was published later in Robert Bistolfi and François Zabbal, eds, *Islams d'Euorpe* (Paris: Éditions de l'Aube, 1995), pp. 230-34. The history of the concept is documented with references in the new rewritten and expanded edition of B. Tibi, *Im Schatten Allahs. Der Islam und die Menschenrechte* (München: Ullstein, 2003), Kap. 12.

first century to avoid "violence, cruelty and political humiliation"[30], which result from a "multiculturalism of fear", a danger of "ethnic politics". I agree with Jacob Levy that this "multiculturalism of fears places perhaps an unusual degree of emphasis on recurrent social and political dangers, which must be avoided, but cannot be escaped."[31] In my Stanford paper[32] I employ this approach in the study of Europe and coin the formula 'ethnicity of fear'. The alternative to it is Euro-Islam.

Questions and Answers

Q. Professor, thank you very much for your fascinating presentation, which I agree with 99%, especially on the issue of the social marginalization of Muslims in Europe. I have one comment. There are twenty million Muslims in Europe and there are four hundred and fifty million Europeans. That's actually quite a small percentage. Do you think that the problems really arise since there are strong concentrations of Islamic communities in a limited number of cities in Europe, and is there something one can do about that? My experience is that most migrants are comfortable with living in - for want of a better expression - ghettos. I'm guilty of that myself. I'm British, and people say: well, you live in a ghetto in Brussels, which is a British ghetto. That's very common among migrant communities. They feel comfortable there, they can get their own food, they have their own restaurants, not that you want to eat British food, particularly in Belgium, but the fact is that migrant communities really like to be together, at least in the initial stages of the migration process. Trying social engineering to move them out never works. It's been tried in Canada, it's been tried in Sweden, and 99% gravitate back to their communities in the cities. I just wondered whether you'd like to comment on that.

A. Yes, the figure is small, but the figure is increasing rapidly, but let's put this aside. The magnitude of the figure, whether it is doubling, tripling, the problem is spatial separation. I'll try to make this clear by one example. The cartoon crisis first started in Copenhagen, and then became European, then global. The imam who was the top

---

[30] Jacob Levy, *The Multiculturalism of Fear* (New York: Oxford University Press, 2000), p. 12.
[31] Ibid., p. 11.
[32] For details see note 16 above.

master of the crisis travelled around the world, and by the end of the conflict the twelve cartoons had become a hundred and twenty, and the cartoons became ever uglier. So there was an orchestration at work. It was reported to me by a reliable source that the imam who orchestrated the crisis warned the prime minister of Denmark: "We are only two hundred and fifty thousand people here, but you are the minority, it is not us the minority". The Minister responded "I do not get it. You live in the Danish society and you need to accommodate to us. We have press freedom. I may not like the cartoons, but I have no authority to censure the people who published the cartoons. Why do you say we are the minority?" He explained to him: "We live in a global world. We are 1.6 billion people and you are only five million." Muslims perceive of themselves as a community, an *Umma*. To put it in Hobsbawm's terminology[33], there's a reinventing of the *Umma*, an imaginary of the *Umma*: if you don't give me an identity as a European, I identify myself with the *Umma*. The problem is not only the spatial segregation, but the self-awareness of the people living in these ghettos. They feel they are not part of Europe, but part of an Islamic *Umma* with a mission to Islamize Europe. I'm speaking here as a Muslim, I want to be European, and I want a place for Islam in Europe. But I would not allow myself, if I wanted to be decent, to say I'm here to Islamize Europe. This is the issue, and therefore the problem is integration. I live in the United States of America since 1982. My home in the US is Boston, and Boston is also ethnically subdivided. But when I meet Hispanics or Chinese, or even Arabs in America, they all say: "I am Chinese-American". In Berlin the Turks don't say: "I'm a German Turk", or "a Turkish German". In America there are about three hundred thousand people of Turkish background and I am quite at home in the Turkish community in the US. There are two differences: the Turks in the US are middle class people, that's why they are integrated. The Turks in Germany are not. This is one problem. The other problem is that German society is not inclusive, but American society is inclusive. I never met a Turk in America who said, "I'm a Turk", even those who do not have an American passport. They say: "I'm American of Turkish background", or "Turkish-American". This is the issue. Of course the spatial segregation is an issue, but it has to be placed in an overall context.

---

[33] E. Hobsbawm and T. Ranger (eds.), *The Invention of Tradition*, Cambridge: Cambridge University Press, 1992.

Q. As a believer in Europe I accept that double allegiance (European-German, European-Belgian and so on) is part of the European concept, as it is also in the European treaties and in the European constitution. You are both German and European. One can be, in this country, Flemish, or Walloon or whatever, so there are dual or triple allegiances. My belief has always been that the weaker a national identity is, the stronger, or the more possible it will be to become a European citizen. Strong national identities, the British or the French, may possibly constitute a hindrance to becoming a European citizen. If that is so and if Islam has a strong identity, as it certainly has, then it would seem to be impossible to Europeanize Islamic citizens. Because it's too strong an identity and a dual identity, a European dual identity will therefore be impossible to acquire. If I may add another question: and that is about European secularism, as you said, which in my view also has gone too far. The question is: if Europe were less secular, would you believe in the inter-religious dialogue, and that European believers might be in a better position to argue and to debate with Islam than European non-believers?

A. I lived 44 years in Europe, that's enough to know that there is European civilization, and there are European values. If you go to southern Italy, people of southern Italy and people from Scandinavia, they are culturally very different, but from the point of view of civilization they share the same old view, some basic values. But if I understand you well, this is a European problem; the awareness of this is very weak. And that's why it is so difficult to make Muslims accept the European identity, since Europeans themselves do not stand up for this identity, or the awareness of this is very weak. Of course there's German, French local identity. You are Belgian, you are European, you are Christian, and this is no contradiction. You combine the three. But when it comes to civic values, they are European, and Muslims have become part of this, but to make this reality requires a joint venture, a joint European-Islamic venture: an *esprit de corps* shared by Muslims and Europeans, and this is a project for the future.

One question about religion. Religion is returning, the term was coined by the Harvard sociologist Daniel Bell, the return of the sacred[34]. The return of the sacred is taking place throughout the world, but not in Europe, except among the migrant communities. I propose you distinguish between secularization and profanation.

---

[34] D. Bell, *The End of Ideology: On the Exhaustion of Political Ideas in the Fifties*, 1960.

This difference is not from me, but also from Daniel Bell. Secularization means separation of religion and politics, which is fine, but profanation means abolishing religion, and the result is that in the end you have no more sacred. People in every culture have the sacred. The sacred could be even worldly, it's not always faith. Among Arabs, what is sacred is honour. Honour is something sacred. Europeans have no sacred anymore. To Middle Easterners and Muslims living in Europe, Europeans have no honour anymore, you can do anything with them. The result is a lack of respect. It is therefore very important for Europeans to understand that secularism is not identical with profanation. Profanation means everything is relative and you accept it in the name of diversity. Mohammed is sacred for Muslims and if you present him as a terrorist, I am insulted. I'm a rational man, I do not want conflict, but when I see Mohammed portrayed as a terrorist with a bomb on his head, I am insulted, because Mohammed is sacred for me. Muslims ask Europeans to respect their sacred. But we also have to respect your sacred, like your constitution, your understanding of democracy. We have no right to touch this. But Europeans do not behave in this manner.

Q. *I have a very practical question. Imagine you were a newcomer in Antwerp, which is in the Flemish part of Belgium. What kind of book would you like to be handed over by the mayor: "Welcome to the Flemish community in Antwerp", or "Welcome as a European citizen"?*

A. European citizen.

Q. *I see two main challenging issues when it comes to setting up a policy that gives Muslims a feeling of belonging to our European societies. The first issue relates to the question: who is a representative spokesman of the Muslim communities? European countries are eagerly looking forward to having such body, institutionalized or not, that can speak on behalf of the Muslim community. And yet another issue is the ignorance on our part of what in Islam is the perception of what should be the position of Muslims in a non-Muslim country. Are they conceived of as pilgrims, are they minorities, are they minorities in the short term, but in the long term entitled to look for the establishment of a Muslim State? What is the status of Muslims in a non-Muslim country in the Islamic view? Are there different views?*

We are ignorant of this issue. To set up a dialogue presupposes that you know of the other's position. I see two very challenging issues here.

A. When it comes to Islam, it is very important to distinguish between the body of Islam as it exists in the *Qur'ân*, the holy book of the Muslims, and the *Hadith*, the tradition of prophet, and what developed after. But Muslims do not draw this line very clearly. Many things were developed after the end of Islamic revelation, from the seventh century on. Muslims, even educated ones, say this is an essential part of Islam. If you change it, this is a problem with us. Europeans have problems with cultural change; Muslims also have problems with cultural change. In Islam, cultural change poses a problem since often people say: "this is from Allah, and I am not entitled to change it, and if you change it, you are changing what Allah prescribes and you become a heretic."

Now how do Muslims view themselves who are living in Europe? I'm not talking about secular Muslims; I'm talking about religious Muslims, even educated ones. In Islam there is the concept of the minority in Islam, and that changed. In the 21st century the minorities in Islam are Christian and Jews, and Islam considers itself to be a tolerant religion, and therefore you have to accommodate Jews and Christians as *dhimmi* – *dhimmi* means protected minorities, but they are second-class citizens. They do not have equal rights with Muslims. But the problem in the 21st century is different: now you have Muslims as minorities, and not only in Europe. In Europe we have twenty million. The largest Islamic minority in the world lives in India. India has a population of one billion people. Thirteen percent are Muslims. That makes 130 million Muslims. Traditionally, minorities in Islam are Jews and Christians, the *Qur'ân* mentions only these religions. In Islamic theology, Hinduism does not exist. The innovation that was introduced by Indian Muslims is to add to these minorities the Indian Muslims. However, the Indian Muslims look at Hindus, who are the majority, as a minority. But the reality is opposite, and so this is a problem. At the university of al Azhar (Cairo) there is a new concept now being developed: secular jurisprudence of minorities. Muslim minorities in Europe have to demand the validity of the *Shari'a*, and they are not allowed to integrate fully, because that would make them loose their religion. This is a theology now being developed. This is not fundamentalism, but I find it threatening, because it is against integration, and it emanates from the authoritative Sunni institution in Islam. In my view, we are a minority, we're living in a secular society and we have to accommodate. This is no contradiction to diversity. If I do not want to accommodate in the name of diversity, then once again we have a problem.

In France, the State has been promoting secular Islam, supporting secular Muslims to the extent possible. Their major spokesman is the imam of the Mosque in Paris, who acknowledges *laïcité* in public and says: "The Muslims living in France must accept the French constitution." And in France they created, on behalf of the State, the *Association Française du Culte Musulman*. In their view the State and civil society in Europe must participate, must have a say in the formation of the representation of Islam. If you don't do that, the fundamentalists will take over. It is not a problem of tolerance. I've been working on political Islam for thirty years. Political Islam is not only an idea, Islamism is not only an idea, it is a transnational movement, globally linked to one another, with an infrastructure, with extremely rich funding, they get millions of funding, and they are in Europe. Ordinary Muslims who are the majority, 90%, have no associations, no federations. If you want someone to talk to, who is organized, you find it in Islamism, but I am afraid this is not the right solution. I am therefore in favour of the French model: the State and civil society claim to have a say in who is representing Islam, and they demand an acknowledgement and also a commitment to the French constitution.

Muslim Integration
and Secularism[1]

Tariq Modood

I believe there is an anti-Muslim wind blowing across the European continent. One factor is the perception that Muslims are making politically exceptional, culturally unreasonable or theologically alien demands upon European states. Against that, I wish to say, that the claims Muslims are making, in fact, parallel comparable arguments about gender or ethnic equality. Seeing the issue in that context shows how European and contemporary is the logic of mainstream Muslim identity politics. Additionally I shall argue that multicultural politics must embrace what I call a moderate secularism, and resist a radical secularism.

My main experience of these issues, both the lived experience, but also in terms of research and intellectual reflection, is based upon Britain, but I believe this experience has relevance beyond Britain. Of course so many of these issues are becoming European issues, for at policy level there is convergence as well as divergence, and moreover our countries impact upon another. We see that so dramatically at the start of 2006, with the Danish cartoon affair, which became a multinational affair, having an impact domestically in a number of countries including those some distance from Denmark.

In Britain we have to come to approach issues to do with Muslim integration through what we used to call – and in other countries the language will not always have a natural resonance or fit – 'race-relations', which is an American term. We are of course talking about the post-war migration of non-Europeans into a European country, or from the global South to the global North. And this phenomenon in Britain, initially at least, was very much understood with American ideas. People saw the issue as primarily one of colour racism, which of course had a historical legacy: slavery, colonialism, empire, and so on. The whole issue to do with Muslims, which is a headline issue today only became a feature of majority-minority relations from the early 1990s. In Britain nobody talked about the Muslims in the 1980s. The big dramatic

---

[1] This chapter is based on my *Multicultural Politics: Racism, Ethnicity and Muslims in Britain* (University of Minnesota Press and University of Edinburgh Press, 2005) and my *Multiculturalism: A Civic Idea* (Polity Press, 2007).

crisis that brought the idea of Muslims into public political discourse was the "Satanic Verses" or the Salman Rushdie affair in 1989-90.

Up to that time, and to some extent beyond that time, the dominant post-immigration issue was colour racism. One consequence of that is that the legal and policy framework in Britain still reflects the conceptualization and priorities of racial dualism, of black-white dualism. Muslims and issues about Muslims arose in that context, and have struggled to seek clarity and a distinctive set of priorities, by counterposing themselves in that context, against that agenda. This dependence upon a 'race' framework has meant, at least initially, that Muslims have been marginalized. To some extent the assertiveness of Muslims in Britain has to be understood in the context of trying to move themselves from a marginalized position where things were seen in terms of black and white, to one where they say "talk to us as Muslims, treat us as Muslims, not just as people who are not white".

Moreover, in this Atlantocentric version of racism, which is certainly one of the classical and enduring versions, phenotype explains the existence of certain cultural traits (Miles 1989: 71-72). These traits are mainly negative in the case of blacks, people of African descent. As a result, racism or racial discrimination comes to be thought of as unfavourable treatment on the grounds of 'colour'. I refer to this as 'colour-racism'. While the physicality of blacks is taken to be enough to fill out the image of them as a group, as a 'race' – as for example, strong, sensual, rhythmical and unintelligent – the racialised image of Asians is not so extensively linked to physical appearance. It very soon appeals to cultural motifs such as language, religion, family structures, exotic dress, cuisine and art forms. These are taken to be part of the meaning of 'Asian' and of why Asians – which in Britain means South Asians – are alien, backward and undesirable. Such motifs are appealed to in excluding, harassing or discriminating against Asians – in both constituting them as a group and justifying negative treatment of them. Muslims too are, indeed, being generalised about in these and other ways in Europe (and elsewhere) at the moment. They are being perceived not just as neighbours, citizens and so on but as Muslims; and it has to be said that many Muslims – like some blacks, Jews, gays, women, Scots etc in parallel situations before them – are vociferously challenging the negative perceptions but not the underlying logic that Muslims are a group. They are responding to the negative perceptions by offering positive images, stories and generalisations about Muslims; less often by saying Muslims are not a group but a variety of individuals, citizens etc. Hence a process of group-formation is well underway.

Why do I call this process 'racialisation' and the negative dimension of it, 'anti-Muslim racism'? Because the 'otherness' or groupness' that is being appealed to and is being developed is connected to the cultural and racial otherness that is connected to European/white peoples' historical and contemporary perception and treatment of people that they perceive to be non-European or non-white. How Muslims are perceived today is both connected to how they have been perceived and treated by European empires and their racial hierarchies, as well as by Christian Islamophobia and the Crusades in earlier centuries (Daniels 1961 and 1967). The images, generalisations and fears have both a continuity as well as a newness. Moreover, these perceptions and treatments overlap with contemporary European/white peoples' attitudes and behaviour towards blacks, Asians, immigrants and so on. The perception and treatment clearly has a religious and cultural dimension but equally clearly it has a phenotypical dimension. Given a number of images – cartoons – of people and asked to pick out a Muslim, most people would have a go and not reply but I do not know what any of these people believe, just as if they were asked to identify Jews they would have a go (though probably less today than in the past – because Jews are becoming de-racialised, normalised as 'white', in some parts of the west).

It is true that 'Muslim' is not a (putative) biological category in the way that 'black' or 'South Asian' or Chinese is. But nor was 'Jew' once: a long, non-linear history of racialisation turned a faith-cum-ethnic group into a 'race'. More precisely, the latter did not so much as replace the former but superimposed itself. No one denied that Jews were a religious community with a distinctive language(s), culture(s) and religion but they also came to be seen as a race – and with horrific consequences. Similarly, Bosnian Muslims were 'ethnically cleansed' by people who were phenotypically, linguistically and culturally the same as themselves because they came to be identified as an 'ethnic' or a 'racial' group. The ethnic cleanser, unlike an Inquistor, wasted no time in finding out what people believed, if and how often they went to a mosque and so on: their victims were 'ethnically' identified as Muslims. My argument is that this same kind of process – though at least so far at a much lower level of violence – is taking place in western Europe and, I would hazard, in the United States, given public support for 'racial profiling' at airports and by security services etc.

The results of such racialisation or ethnicisation is not 'pure' racism, *i.e.,* it is not just biological or phenotypical, which it might be said to be in the case of people of African descent. But it is clear here that Muslims are not exceptional, as the above example of the Jews illustrates. As I have already suggested, the same is true of the most numerous non-whites in the UK, namely people of south Asian origin, locally called 'Asians' (and less pleasant monikers). I have argued that even before the rise of a distinct anti-Muslim racism there was an anti-Asian racism and that it was distinct from anti-black racism in having distinct stereotypes (if one was unintelligent, aggressive, happy-go-lucky and lazy, the other was 'too clever by half', passive, worked too hard and did not know how to have fun). Moreover, if in the case of black people the stereotypes appealed to some (implicit) biology, to IQ, physical prowess, sense of rhythm, sexual drive and so on, none of the main stereotypes about Asians even implicitly referred to a scientific or folk biology. The stereotypes all referred to Asian cultural norms and community structures – to gender roles and norms, patriarchy, family authority and obligations, arranged marriages, religion, work ethic and so on. So anti-Asian racism is best understood as cultural racism. The most violent form of racism that Asians in Britain have experienced is random physical attacks in public places, 'Paki-bashing'. I have not seen any analysis of this phenomenon that refers to any biological beliefs held by the perpetrators. Interviews with the pool of people from which the perpetrators come – young working-class white males, especially 'skinheads' – and others in their neighbourhoods accuse Asians not of a deficient biology but of being aliens, of not belonging to 'our country', of 'taking over the country' and so on (Bonnett 1993: 19-20; Cohen, 1988: 83; Back, 1993). Actually, of things that the Nazis accused Jews of (as well as of not having the right biology) (Meer and Noorani, in press, 2008).

Once we break with the idea that (contemporary) racism is only about biology or that racism is of one classical kind, then the idea of a pure racism should lose its social science appeal. We should be able to see that cultural groups and religious groups can be racialised; that Muslims can be the victims of racism qua Muslims as well as qua Asians or Arabs or Bosnians. Indeed that these different kinds of racisms can interact and have a dynamic and so can mutate and new forms of racism can emerge (Modood 2005: 6-18 and chp 1). Up to that time, and to some extent beyond that time, the dominant post-immigration issue in Britain was colour racism. One consequence of that is that the legal and policy framework in Britain still reflects the conceptualization and priorities of racial dualism, of black-white dualism. Muslims and issues about Muslims have been born in that context, and have struggled to seek clarity and a distinctive set of priorities, by counter posing themselves in that context, against that agenda. But it has meant, at least initially, that Muslims have been marginalized. To some extent the assertiveness of Muslims in Britain has to be understood in the context of trying to move themselves from a marginalised position where things were seen in terms of black and white, to one where they say "talk to us as Muslims, treat us as Muslims, not just as people who are not white" (*cf.* the British Muslim magazine, *Q-News*; Bari, 2005). The major issue in which this was first crystallised was the protest against Salman Rushdie's novel, *The Satanic Verses*, at the end of the 1980s, when larger numbers of Muslims were mobilised than hitherto had been in relation to racism, and which received very little support from other non-whites (Modood 1990 and 2005)

Identity Politics

The second American influence I want to draw to your attention, is the idea of positive identity. The colour-blind humanism of Martin Luther King Jr., whose philosophy could be expressed as "black, white, we're all the same under the skin", came to be mixed with an emphasis by some of his young successors on black pride, black autonomy, and so on. A similar development has taken place in Britain. We moved from thinking of issues to do with race or 'coloured' minorities as just something to do with skin-colour to people wanting to affirm certain marginalized or suppressed identities. Or people creating new identities, manufacturing identities as a way of negotiating a position of equality and dignity for themselves in the contemporary context.

I think it's best to see the development of what one might call racial explicitness and positive blackness – that is to say people saying "I am black" as opposed to us pretending that equality means that we never notice whether people are black or white – as part of a wider socio-political climate which is not confined to race and culture, or non-white minorities. Feminism, gay-pride, various kinds of minority nationalism in Europe are all examples of new identity movements, which have become an important feature in many countries. Especially in those countries in which class politics has declined in salience. Some of these identities have a territorial face such as Flemish, Basque, Scottish or Quebecois, but there are other movements that don't talk about a territory: gender identity, gay-pride, and ethnic minority identities for example. These identities have become particularly marked in Anglophone countries. In fact it would be fair to say that what is often claimed today in the name of racial equality, again especially in the English speaking world, goes beyond the claims that were made in the 1960s. Iris Young, the American feminist philosopher, expressed well the new political climate, when she described the emergence of an ideal of equality, based not just on allowing excluded groups to assimilate and live by the norms of dominant groups, but on the view that "a positive self-definition of group difference is in fact more liberatory". (1990: 57). So this is a difference-affirming notion of equality, rather than a kind of "we're all the same under the colour of the skin" notion of equality. And this significant shift, from colour-blindness to difference assertion, takes us from an understanding of equality in terms of individualism and cultural assimilation to a politics of recognition, recognition of other identities, to equality as encompassing public ethnicity. This perception of equality means not having to hide or apologize for ones origins, family or community, and requires others to show respect for them. Public attitude and arguments must adapt, so that this heritage is encouraged, not contemptuously expected to wither away.

So we have here two concepts of equality which can be stated as follows: firstly the right to assimilate to the majority or dominant culture in the public sphere, with toleration of difference in the private sphere. The second concept of equality is the right to have one's difference like minority ethnicity, recognized and supported in both the public and the private sphere. While the first represents a classical liberal response to difference, the latter is very much the take of the new identity politics. The two are not however alternative conceptions of equality in the sense that to hold one the other must be rejected. Multiculturalism properly construed requires support for both conceptions, so we're not having to choose between one or the other, but expanding from the first to include the second. The assumption behind the first is that participation in the public or national culture is necessary for the effective exercise of citizenship. The only obstacle to which are the exclusionary processes preventing gradual assimilation. The second conception too assumes that groups excluded from the national culture have their citizenship diminished as a result, and sees the remedy not in rejecting the right to assimilate, but in adding the right to widen and adapt the national culture and the public and media symbols of national membership to include the relevant minority identities. It can be seen then, that the public-private distinction is crucial to the contemporary discussion of equal citizenship and particularly to the challenge of an earlier liberal position. It is in this political and intellectual climate, namely a climate in which what would earlier have been called private matters have become sources of equality struggles, that Muslim assertiveness emerged as a domestic political phenomenon. In this respect the advances achieved by anti-racism and feminism, with its slogan "the personal is the political", acted as a benchmarks for later political group entrants, such as Muslims. I would like to show that while Muslims raise distinctive concerns, the logic of their demands often mirrors those of other equality seeking groups. So one of the current conceptions of equality is difference-affirming equality, with related notions of respect, recognition and identity, and this is what I understand by political multiculturalism. (Modood 2007).

Religious Equality

Now what kinds of specific policy demands are being made by or on behalf of religious groups and Muslim identity politics in particular, when these multiculturalist ideas are deployed? I suggest that these political demands, which I put under the rubric "religious equality" have three dimensions, which as it were, get progressively thicker. They start off minimally but in getting bigger and bigger, they are progressively less acceptable to radical secularists. Very briefly these three sets of demands are firstly, that there should not be religious discrimination. That is the easiest to understand and presumably very few people will want to disagree with it. For instance, an employer should not prefer a candidate, or disfavour a candidate on the basis of that person being of a particular religious background, or of no religious background (except where a religion is a genuine occupational qualification). The next step up in the demand for religious equality is even-handedness in relation to native religion. By this I mean that newly settled religious groups, like Muslims, Hindus, Sikhs and so on, will say "If protestants or Catholics or Jews are allowed certain access to resources or certain institutional representation, then this should be extended to the new religions. 'Even-handedness' (Carens 2000) captures this sense of equality because of course, there will always be some difference of scale; for instance Christians might form 75% of the population, Muslims might form 4% of the population. We can not have a numerical equality, but even-handedness means treating both sets of groups in the same way, in terms of their recognition, in terms of their rights to enjoy public space, public resources such as the school system, the delivery of welfare services, provision in relation to hospitals and the army and so on. Thirdly, religious equality might mean the idea of positive inclusion of religious groups. That would be quite a thick idea of equality, but – and this is my argument – it parallels the claims that are made in relation to gender equality, racial equality and so on. It is not a distinctively religious argument, let alone a distinctively Islamic argument. The basic idea is that we measure equality in society by a number of ways, but one way is by the degree to which all people, regardless of religious background, are equally represented as the recipients of the benefits and opportunities that society has to offer. In Britain, borrowing from the United States, for decades now, we have what we call "ethnic monitoring". That is to say, we record some kind of ethnic self-definition of, for example, candidates for jobs, and we compare that to their success rate in getting jobs, to see whether being, let's say African-Caribbean, has any impact on the likelihood of, say, their being employed in the national health service, or the police, or a university and so on. So, if we do that for race and gender, and of course gender is monitored in this way across most of the countries of the European Union, then why should we not do that for religious groups? Let me give you a very specific example: the BBC currently believes it is of political importance to review and improve its personnel practices and its output programmes, including its on-screen representation of the British population by making provision for, and winning the competence of three particular categories of people. For a few years now various policies have been targeted at improving the position in relation to three particular population groups: women, ethnic groups and young people. Why should it not also use religious groups as a criterion of inclusivity, and help to demonstrate that it is doing the same for viewers and staff defined by religious community membership? That would really then be taking religion as a measure of inclusivity, just as we take these other measures.

Implications for Liberal Citizenship

The multiculturalism or politics of difference that I am advocating has four major implications for liberal citizenship. Firstly, it is clearly a collective project, and concerns collectivities, and not just individuals. Secondly, it is not colour-, gender-, sexual orientation-blind, and so breeches the liberal public-private identity distinction, which prohibits the recognition of particular group identities. Thirdly, it takes race, sex and sexuality beyond being merely ascriptive sources of identity. For liberal citizenship, race is of interest, only because no one can choose their race, and so should not be discriminated against on something over which they have no control. This is the classical liberal position. But if equality is about celebrating previously demeaned identities, and most of our equality discourse is of that kind today, for example, in taking pride in ones blackness, rather than in accepting it merely as a private matter, then what is being addressed in anti-discrimination or promoted as a public identity, is a chosen response to one's ascription, it is not merely an ascriptive category. Exactly the same applies to sex and sexuality: we may not choose our sex or sexual orientation, but we choose how to live with it politically. Do we keep it private, or do we make it the basis of a social movement, and seek public resources and representation for it? Some gay people say "yes", other people say "no", so a public identity has a certain element of choice; it's not merely ascriptive.

That leads me then to the fourth point which is in fact felt by liberals to be the greatest challenge. Muslims and other religious groups are now utilising the kind of identity recognition arguments I have been discussing and claiming religious identity, just like gay identity, and just like certain forms of racial identity, should not just be privatised and tolerated, but should be part of the public space. In their case, however, they come into conflict with an additional fourth dimension of liberal citizenship that we can refer to by 'secularism'. By secularism I mean the view that religion is a feature, perhaps uniquely, of private, not public identity. It expresses itself in the response that women, black and gay, are ascribed, unchosen identities, while being a Muslim is a chosen belief; once you start talking about a religious identity like Muslim, you're no longer talking about the politics of recognition, difference and equality, because all those things (gender, sexuality, race), are chosen, whereas religion is something one can walk away from. I think this extreme secularist response is sociologically naïve, and to some extent it's a political con, a political bad faith argument, because the position of Muslims in countries like ours today is similar to the other identities of difference, as Muslims catch up with and engage with the contemporary culture of equality. No one chooses to be or not to be born into a Muslim family. Similarly, no one chooses to be born into a society where to be a Muslim, or to look like a Muslim creates suspicion, hostility or a failure to get the job you applied for. Though how Muslims respond to these circumstances will vary. Some will organize resistance, while others will try to stop looking like Muslims, the equivalent for what in America has been called 'passing for white'. Some will build an ideology out of their subordination, others will not, just as a woman can choose to be a feminist or not. Again, some Muslims may define their Islam in terms of piety rather than in terms of politics, just as some women may see no politics in their gender, while for others their gender will be at the centre of their politics. So my argument is that we should include Muslims in this arena of marginalized identities that are claiming equality and public space. There is not a category division between gender, race, ethnicity, sexuality on the one hand, and say, Muslims on the other. Those who see the current Muslim assertiveness as an unwanted and illegitimate child of multiculturalism have only two choices if they want to be consistent: they can repudiate the idea of equality as identity recognition, and return to the 1960's liberal idea of equality as colour-, sex-, religion-blindness. (Barry 2001). If it is the latter that is adopted, then it should be consistent with gender-blindness, colour-blindness, with sexual orientation-blindness, not merely single out religion. Or at least we need an explicit argument that equality as recognition does not apply to oppressed religious communities, perhaps uniquely not to religious communities. To deny Muslims positive equality without one of these two arguments is to be open to the charge of double standards. Hence, a programme of racial and multicultural equality is not I believe possible today without a discussion of the merits and limits of secularism. Secularism can no longer be treated as 'off limits', or as former president Jacques Chirac said in a major speech in 2004, 'non-negotiable'.

Secularisms

Not that it's really a matter of being for or against secularism, that's too simple, but rather a careful, institution by institution analysis, of how to draw the public-private boundary and further the cause of multicultural equality and inclusivity. For this public-private boundary is not as simple as it seems. What seems appropriate in one country can be regarded as very inappropriate in another country. While all western countries are clearly secular in many ways, their interpretations of secularisms and the institutional arrangements which give substance to it diverge according to the dominant national religious culture, and the different projects of nation-state building. So it may be a universal idea, but it takes a number of not just different but contradictory forms. For example, the United States' first amendment to the constitution, that there shall be no established church has wide support in that country; and in the last two decades, there has been a tendency amongst academics and jurists to interpret the church-State separation in continually more radical ways (Sandel 1994; Hamburger, 2002). Yet, as is well known, not only is the US a deeply religious society with much higher levels of church attendance than in western Europe, but there is a strong protestant, even evangelical fundamentalism, that is rare in Europe. This fundamentalism disputes some of the new radical interpretations of the 'no establishment' clause, though not necessarily the clause itself. And it is one of the primary mobilising forces in American politics. It is widely claimed that it decided the presidential elections of 2004. The churches in question – mainly white, mainly in the South and Midwest – campaign openly for candidates and parties, indeed raise large sums of money for politicians, and introduce religion-based issues into politics, such as positions on abortion, HIV-Aids, homosexuality, stem cell-research, prayer at school and so on. It is said that no openly avowed atheist has ever been a candidate for the White House, and that it would be impossible for such a candidate to be elected. It is not at all unusual for politicians, in fact for president George W. Bush it's most usual, to publicly talk about their faith, to appeal to religion, and to hold prayer meetings in government buildings. On the other hand, in 'establishment' Britain bishops sit in the upper chamber of the legislature by right, and only the senior Archbishop can crown a new head of state, the monarch, yet politicians rarely talk about their religion. British politicians exercise a reticence and guard a privacy about religion which is seen to be part of the profession of politics. It was noticeable for example, that when Prime Minister Blair went to a summit meeting with President Bush to discuss aspects of the Iraq War in 2003, the US media widely reported that the two leaders had prayed together. Yet Prime Minister Blair, one of the most openly professed and active Christian ever to hold that office, refused to answer questions on this issue from the British media on his return, saying it was a private matter. So what in America is regarded perfectly fine for presidents to do, in Britain, the Prime Minister says "this is a private matter, you have no right to ask me". The British State may have an established church, but the beliefs of the Queen's First Minister are his own concern.

France draws the distinction between State and religion differently again. Like the US, there's no State church, but unlike the US, the State actively promotes the privatisation of religion. While in the US organized religion in civil society is powerful and seeks to exert influence on the political process, French civil society does not carry signs or expressions of religion. Yet the French State, contrary to the US, confers institutional legal status on the Catholic and Protestant churches, and on the Jewish consistory, albeit carefully designating organized religion as 'cultes' and not communities. So, we have a situation where in England or Britain, we have a very weak establishment and religion is weak in civil society, but not absent – it can lead campaigns for nuclear disarmament, third world debt relief, peace movements and so on. In the US, establishment is constitutionally prohibited, but religion is strong and is politically mobilised. And then thirdly, in France, we have an actively secular State, which offers top-down recognition, and yet religion is weak in civil society – indeed, in many ways, it is kept out of civil society.

	State	**Religion in Civil Society**
England/ Britain	Weak establishment but churches have a political voice	Weak but churches can be a source of political criticism and action
United States	No establishment	Strong and politically mobilized
France	Actively secular but offers top-down recognition/control	Weak and it is rare for churches to be political

Modood 2007, previously adapted from Modood and Kastoryano, 2006.

Table 1. Religion vis-à-vis State and Civil Society in three Countries From

So, given this kind of diversity, which is not confined to the three cases discussed here (the diversity gets more and more multiple the more cases we look at), what are the appropriate limits of the State? It seems that we can all be good secularists but disagree on what are the appropriate limits of the State. Everyone will agree that there should be religious freedom, and that this should include freedom of belief and worship in private associations. That is more or less a universal position excluding a few places like Saudi Arabia, which of course does not claim to be a secular polity. Family too falls on the private side of the line, but the State regulates the limits of what is a lawful family. For example, polygamy is not permitted in many countries, not to mention the deployment of official definitions of family in the distribution of welfare-entitlement. Religions typically put a premium on mutuality, on mutual aid, and on care of the sick, the homeless, the elderly and so on. They set up organizations to pursue these aims, but so do States. Should there be a competitive or cooperative relationships between these religions and State organisations, or do they have to ignore each other? Can public money, raised out of taxes on religious as well as non-religious citizens not be used to support the organisations favoured by some religious taxpayers? What of schools? Do parents not have the right to expect that schools, while pursuing border educational civic aid, will make an effort not to create a conflict between the work of the school, and the upbringing of the children at home, but rather show respect for their religious background? Can parents, as associations of religious citizens, not set up their own schools, and should those schools not be supported out of the taxes of the same parents? Is the school where the private meets the public, or is it in some platonic manner, where the state takes over the children from the family, and pursues its own purposes? Even if there is to be no established church, the state may still wish to work with organized religion as social partner, as in the case of Germany, or to have some forum in which it consults with organized religion, some kind of national council of religions, as in Belgium. Or even if it does not do that, because it is regarded as compromising the principle of secularism, political parties, being agents in civil society, rather than organs of the State, may wish to do this, and institute special representation for religious groups, as many do for groups defined by age, gender, region, language, ethnicity, and so on. What is wrong, for example, with having a Muslim section of the Labour Party, or the Christian Democrat Party? Why is that a breach of principles but not when we do this for other identity groups?

It is clear then, that the idea of the public is a multifaceted concept, and in relation to secularism, may be defined differently in relation to different dimensions of religion and in different countries? We can all be secularists then, all approve of secularism in some respect, and yet have quite different views, influenced by historical legacies and varied pragmatic compromises of where to draw the line between the public and the private, because these lines are often pragmatic, they're not simply deduced from an abstract principle. It would be quite mistaken to suppose that all religious spokespersons or at least all political Muslims are on one side of the line, wherever that line is, and all others are on the other side. There are many different ways of drawing the various lines of that issue. In the past, the drawing of them had reflected particular contexts, shaped by differential customs, urgency of needs, and sensitivity to the sensibilities of the relevant religious groups. Where the lines are in Belgium, or the Netherlands or in Britain, has not been arrived at by an abstract ethical principle, blind to society. They have been made to work by working with the sensibilities of the relevant populations. Exactly the same consideration of relevance and sensitivity is needed in relation to the accommodation of Muslims in Europe, not a battle of slogans and ideological oversimplification. So, multicultural equality, when applied to religious groups, means that secularism, *simpliciter* appears to be an obstacle to pluralistic integration and equality. But secularism pure and simple is not what exists in the world. So the obstacle is just an ideological or an imaginary obstacle. The country-by-country situation is, as we have seen, more complex and indeed far less inhospitable to the accommodation of Muslims than the ideology of secularism might suggest.

Let me summarize the approach that I think we should take. Firstly, I am arguing for a reconceptualization of equality from sameness to an incorporation of respect for difference. Secondly, I am arguing for a reconceptualization of secularism from the concept of neutrality and a strict public-private divide to a moderate and evolutionary secularism, based on institutional adjustments which takes account of the sensibilities of religious people and so varies from country to country. Thirdly, let us take a pragmatic, case by case, negotiated approach to dealing with controversy and conflict as it arises, because this is what we have done historically, and not some kind of ideological view that says Muslim demands are unreasonable because they breach some fundamental principle of secularism. So this institutional integration approach is based on including Islam into the institutional framework of the state, using the historical accommodation between state and church as a basis for negotiation, in order to achieve consensual resolutions, consistent with equality and justice. As these accommodations have varied from country to country, it means there is no exemplary solution, for contemporary solutions too will depend on the national context, and will not have a once and for all time basis, because we are actually always revising these matters. It is clearly a dialogical perspective and assumes the possibility of mutual education and learning. The recognition of Islam in Europe can take a corporatist form, can be lead or even imposed by the state in a top-down way, and therefore can take a church or ecclesiastical model as its form, and I think it does sometimes. This may be appropriate for certain countries at certain moments, and could be, usually is, consistent with the conception of multiculturalism. However, it's not ideal, and it would not be my own preference. For example it would not represent the British multicultural experience and its potentiality at its best. Incorporate inclusion would require Muslims and their representatives to speak with one voice, when that is not typical of at least Sunni Islam, and certainly is not typical for South-Asian Sunni Islam as practiced by a majority of Muslims in Britain. My own preference would be for an approach that is less corporatist, less statist and less churchy, in brief, less French. Because I think that is what's typical of the French model, that it's corporatist, statist and actually very churchy, even though the French think they have secularism at the heart of it. An approach in which civil society played a greater role would be more comfortable with there being a variety of Muslim voices, representatives and groups. Different institutions, organisations and associations would seek to accommodate Muslims in ways that worked for them best at a particular time, knowing that these ways may, or ought to be modified over time and Muslim and other pressure groups and civic actors may be continually evolving their claims and agendas. Improvisation, flexibility, consultation, learning by –to use American expression- 'suck it and see' and by the example of others, incrementalism, and all the other virtues of a pragmatic politics in close touch with a dynamic civil society can as much and perhaps better, bring about multicultural equality, than a top-down corporatist inclusion. So representation here would mean the inclusion of a diversity of backgrounds and sensibilities, not delegates or corporate structures. Recognition then, must be pragmatically and experimentally handled, and civil society must share the burden of representation. In my preferred approach it would be quite likely that different kinds of groups, Muslims, Hindus and Catholics for instance, let alone women, gays and different ethnic minority groups, might choose to organize in different ways, and to relate to key civic and political institutions in different ways. While each might look over its shoulders at what the others are doing or getting, and use any such precedent to formulate its own claims, we should on this approach not require symmetry, but be able to live with some degree of what we might call variable geometry. I'm unable to specify what this degree of flexibility might be, but it should be clear that sensitivity to the specific religious, cultural and socio-economic needs in a specific time and place, in a political context, is critical to multiculturalism. This indeterminacy leaves something to be desired, but I hope it is evident that it can be a strength too. It also underlines that multiculturalism is not a comprehensive political theory, but can and must sit alongside other political values and be made to work with varied institutional, national and historical contexts.

So, just a few words of conclusion. The emergence of Muslim political agency has thrown British multiculturalism – and its European equivalents – into theoretical and practical disarray. It has led to policy reversals in the Netherlands and elsewhere, and across Europe has strengthened intolerant, exclusive nationalism. We should in fact be moving the other way, and enacting the kinds of legal and policy measures that are necessary to accommodate Muslims as equal citizens in European politics. These would include anti-discrimination measures in areas such as employment, positive action to achieve a full and just political representation of Muslims in various areas of public life, the inclusion of Muslim history as European history, and so on, it would include all these things. Critically, I've been arguing that the inclusion of Islam as an organized religion, and of Muslim identity as a public identity are necessary to integrate Muslims and to pursue religious equality. While this inclusion runs against certain interpretations of secularism, it is not inconsistent with what secularism means in practice in Europe. We should let this evolving moderate secularism, and the spirit of compromise it represents be our guide. Unfortunately an ideological secularism is currently being asserted especially by central-left intellectuals and generating European domestic versions of what one might call the clash of civilization. That some people are today developing secularism as an ideology to oppose Islam and its public recognition, is a challenge both to pluralism and equality, and thus to some of the bases of contemporary democracy. It has to be resisted no less than, say, the radical anti-secularism of some Islamist.

References

Bari, A. (2005). *Race, Religion and Multiculturalism.* London: Renaissance Press.
Barry, B (2001). *Culture Equality,* Cambridge: Polity Press.
Back, L. (1993). 'Race, Identity and Nation within an Adolescent Community in South London'. *New Community,* 19(2), 217-233.
Bonnett, A. (1993). *Radicalism, Anti-Racism and Representation.* London/New York: Routledge.
Carens, J. (2000). *Culture, Citizenship and Community: A Contextual Exploration of Justice as Evenhandedness.* Oxford: Oxford University Press.
Cohen, P. (1988). 'The Perversions of Inheritance: Studies in the Making of Multi-racist Britain', in P. Cohen and H.S. Bains (eds.), *Multi-Racist Britain.* London: Macmillan.
Daniels, N. (1961). *Islam and the West.* Vol. 1, *Making of an Image, 1000-1300 A.D.* Edinburgh: Edinburgh University Press.
Daniels, N. (1967). *Islam and the West.* Vol. 2, *Islam, Europe and Empire.* Edinburgh: Edinburgh University Press.
Hamburger, P. (2002). *Separation of Church and State.* Cambridge, Mass: Harvard University Press.
Meer, N., and Noorani, T. (forthcoming, 2008). 'A comparison of anti-Semitism and anti-Muslim sentiment in Britain'. *Sociological Review.*
Miles, R. (1989). *Racism.* London and New York: Routledge.
Modood, T. (1990). 'British Asian Muslims and the Rushdie Affair'. *The Political Quarterly,* vol. 61, no. 2, 143–160.
Modood, T. (2005). *Multicultural Politics: Muslims, Ethnicity and Racism in Britain.* Minnesota and Edinburgh Universities Presses.
Modood, T. (2007). *Multiculturalism: A Civic Idea.* Oxon, U.K.: Polity Press.
Modood, T. and Kastoryano, R (2006). 'Secularism and the Accommodation of Muslims in Europe', in T. Modood, A. Triandafyllidou and R. Zapata-Barrero (eds.), *Multiculturalism, Muslims and Citizenship: A European Approach*: London: Routledge.
Sandel, M. (1994). 'Review of Rawls' Political Liberalism'. *Harvard Law Review,* 107: 1765-1794.
Young, I.M. (1990). *Justice and the Politics of Difference.* Princeton, N.J.: Princeton University Press.

Questions and Answers

Q. *We both agree that there is a kind of anti-Muslim wind blowing across Europe. However, when I try to explain this problem to some of my colleagues, I feel that it is not easy to explain, because there is a risk of misunderstanding. For example, when a Western European speaks of racism, he means racism based on skin, and he or she will argue that there is no such thing anymore because we all have black friends and colleagues and so on. On the other hand I feel that many Muslims experience a sort of religious, cultural racism. My question is: could it be that there is a shift from a biological form of racism to a more cultural and religious kind of racism, and if so, how do we deal with it? Because once we drop the term "racism", discussion becomes nearly impossible, since we accuse people of a very serious mistake.*

A. Yes, there's a book by an American author: "I'm not a racist, but...". I would say that I'm one of the people who think that the ways in which Muslims are treated in our countries is a form of racism. Why do I think that? I've basically got two kinds of answers, and they're complementary. One is practical and contextual, and the other one is more theoretical. The practical and contextual is really to do with the way that I told my story. Because I was telling the British story, I started with the idea of race, race inequality, race discrimination, colour racism and so on. When we had the post-war migration from places like the West Indies, the Caribbean, to Britain, many people, many white British people, as well as actually quite a lot of black people, looked at the American experience as a historical template, saying "Oh, we don't want London to be like New York", and so they assumed that the issues were to do with colour racism, and to some extent they got it right, they were. So we borrowed this idea of racism, we began to act on it quite early on, so the British legislation in relation to racial discrimination goes back to the 1960's and has been strengthened subsequently. People like me, I mean I actually worked in the Commission for racial equality for a while, but my family is from Pakistan, I could feel that I wasn't captured in the kind of black/white analysis of race relations. It had an Asian character. It had a Muslim dimension, that was not being captured either theoretically by the academics, by the anti-racists, the legislators, the policy-makers and so on. And so I very strongly argue that we must see the experiences that include Indians, Pakistanis, Bangladeshi, and that therefore are not confined to Muslims. We must see that experience as a form of cultural racism. What is really interesting are two things. Firstly, in Britain for a long period of time, our data have shown that there is more hostility to people of South Asian origin than to people of African descent. Initially the gap was quite small, but recently it's widened. So no one can deny that South Asians are suffering some kind of hostility, whether we call it racism or not. But if you look at the stereotypes that people have about South Asians, and that for instance police will use, or that an employer will use in discriminating, there are things like: "Asians are hard workers, but they are devious, they stick to their own. They are intelligent, brainy, but they lack personal social skills, they would make very bad managers, but they'll make good technicians and technologists and so on. They are oppressive in terms of gender relations. They can be really just fanatics, they are just too family-centred". Now that's half a dozen stereotypes that we have in British society. What is interesting about all those stereotypes is that not one of them relates to biology, but everybody knows that South Asians will be discriminated on the basis of their appearance, or when they send in an application form, just by someone noting a name, like you now "Randid Singh". So we all think there is discrimination against South Asians on the base of colour, no one denies that, we all believe that, social science has gathered evidence, but we know that it's not just colour, that the discriminator has something in mind that cannot be captured by a classical idea of racism as biology, as behaviour determined by biological traits. So people like me have coined the term "cultural racism" to help to explain this kind of two-step, i.e. that you identify a group of people on the basis of their appearance, but actually what's working against that person as a group member are cultural stereotypes, stereotypes that denigrate that person's cultural background. You're still racializing that group, because you're still saying "they are a group", and of course a group that may have exceptions. The number of people who have told me: "oh, of course, you're not like them, you're not like the Asians I'm talking about", or when they say something about Muslims, they say "Tariq, I don't mean you, of course". You racialize the group, even if you make exceptions, but all stereotypes admit exceptions. That's what we mean by cultural racism: you identify a group by their appearance, so all the legacy of phenotype does the work of "othering" that group, and then you load these stereotypes with derogatory cultural attributes. That's cultural racism, and to some extent Britain has moved from colour racism predominance to cultural racism predominance, although we have both and have always had both. And in this respect we have come closer to Europe, because I think the dominant racism in Europe is much more cultural racism than colour racism, and has been for decades, so you've been decades "ahead" of us. France I think is a very good example, where you have black francophones, especially from the Caribbean or from West Africa, who are regarded as, you know, "good French", good French guys and women, and can even be members of the Front National. But Arabs, oh no! Arabs are defined in terms of cultural traits, but identified on the basis of their appearance. So France is a classic case of cultural racism. The dominant racism in Europe now is a form of cultural racism, and the dominant group it's targeted against are Muslim. But the person who does the targeting can be quite ignorant. So one of the consequences of that, in Britain, is that non-Muslims can suffer anti-Muslim discrimination. For example the Sikhs: Sikh men, those who are orthodox, wear a turban, and they're not allowed to cut their hair, so they roll it up and wear a turban, and have a long beard. They actually look more like Osama Bin Laden than I do. So when there's anti-Muslim hostility, lots of Sikhs get shouted at on public transport and in public places: "go back to Osama Bin Laden", or "you Muslims", and Sikh temples get anti-Muslim graffiti written onto them. So a lot of Asian people who are Hindus and Sikhs complain: "why are we getting it? These Muslims should be getting it, not us". In sum, anti-Muslim racism can target anyone who looks like a Muslim, because we do not at the moment wear yellow triangles and stars and so on. So, people don't know who the Muslims are.

Q. *Knowing that, what kind of policy should we set up to address this problem?*

A. What I've been arguing for in Britain over something like fifteen years is that the first thing we need to do is to have an accurate analysis. So the accurate analysis would take the form that we don't see racism in black-white terms, that we don't think that racism is about biological determinism. Because once you say racism is about biology, nearly everybody could say: "I'm not a racist". Most people know nothing about biology anyway, so if you said to them: "what is it that makes black people inferior?" they've got no answer. We need an accurate, sociologically sophisticated analysis of racism. The second step would be to recognize that there's not one racism, there are racisms, it's a plural phenomenon, because all the stereotypes I gave you about south Asians are actually a total opposite of stereotypes about black people. If Asians are hard working, black people are lazy; if black people are unintelligent, Asians are too brainy, or, to use an English expression, are "too clever by half", which means they're clever at getting around you, but you shouldn't trust them; if black people can't maintain basic family unity and family structure, Asians are too family obsessed, "why are they always going on about their families?" Asian people just don't mix, black people are very sociable, too sociable, one group's too sociable, the other's not sociable enough. So there are racisms, we make the demographic generalizations about groups, we don't have a single list of what the other is, there are a number of different others, and then of course that means that remedies must be targeted. We mustn't have an idea that a single set of solutions, a single set of remedies will work for every group. Because if it's true that the problem is diverse, the solutions might be diverse. Very specifically what I've been arguing for in Britain, and we were moving in this direction till at least 2001, now we're zigzagging around, there's a lot more confusion now, that we must have explicit anti-discrimination measures to do with religion. We mustn't just rely on race and ethnicity to do the work, we must have the inclusion of Muslims, and that kind of explicit inclusion in the way that I was arguing for in my talk. Those are the kinds of things that we need to do, if we need to actually be sociologically sophisticated and up to date in our analysis of problems.

Q. *My home city Antwerp is known for a traditional tolerance towards Jews. We used to have 40,000 and now we have 80,000, and we live with them in peace, and we find them a little bit funny, but they are tolerated, while at the same time it's one of the most anti-Muslim cities. What is the reason that one group is tolerated so well and not the other? Is it due to tradition, history, or are there economic reasons?*

A. I don't know the case of Antwerp, your city. What I do know is that historical studies of Britain show that so many of the things that are said about recently arrived groups in Britain, have been said about other groups when they arrived, but now nobody thinks that of them. Jewish people now in Britain, they're quite a small group really, less than half a percent of the population, they are a very prosperous, professional, well-established group. When they first came, say at the turn of the nineteenth into the twentieth century, the time of the pogroms in Eastern Europe and Russia and so on, there's lots of historical work to show that English people who received them, London for instance, said that they were dirty, smelly, unhygienic. That they didn't have Christian values, that they were stuck in ways that Britain had gone beyond, they were backwards in terms of gender relations, that there were too many of them, they had too many large families, they stuck together, they traded with each other, they kept their business for themselves, and therefore they as it were had reverse discrimination against other people, and they had the wrong kind of politics, because too many of them were involved with communists and anarchists, and that they were nationally alien. Of course they couldn't speak English, and so they spoke to each other in some kind of babble of their own. All of the things that are said about recent arrivals were said about their predecessors, whether it was fifty years ago, a hundred years ago, a hundred and fifty years ago and so on. And not just the Jews, but also the Irish coming to England to help in the industrial revolution economy, to help build the roads in England and so on, they had all these things said about them. So the first thing I would say is that time makes the difference, not the group. Somehow the Jews are nice and cuddly and Muslims are not, that's not the issue. I don't even think it's to do with the fact that one is more economically threatening than the other *per se*, because of course that's a factor of time. Jews were seen to be economically threatening, and trade unions for instance didn't want Jewish people coming into the country, because they thought it would bring wages down, that they would be cheap labour, which is an argument we hear again today. Other people didn't like them because they set up their own businesses which were then more successful than their local rivals. So what lessons to draw from that, I suppose actually one could be optimistic and say that we needn't be defeated. Did you want to come in with something?

Q. *I refer to your concept of secularism and equality and the dialogue concept. What kind of Muslim community organization is in your view necessary in a State like Great Britain or in Europe? A Muslim council, whether elected or not, would that be another type of framework?*

A. I guess I would begin with: how did Britain do things before there were any Muslims, and what would be an appropriate extension of current ways of working of what we think is democratic consultation and that would include Muslims? Our political parties, even our centre right party, like the Conservative party, no longer believe in what one might call colour blindness or gender blindness. Even the socialists used to say "we must be blind to difference, all citizens are the same", a single-minded republicanism. Today they don't say that anymore. Even the Conservative party says "we want to increase the number of ethnic minority people in our party, we want to increase the number of ethnic minority people from our party who get elected at every level in the country, and in parliament." So I would say that, if that's alright for women and ethnic minorities, maybe then it's all right to have Muslims. We shouldn't object if, and that's an if, Muslims in the Conservative party or Labour party or somewhere else say "actually we can make a better contribution to our political party if you give us some space to organize ourselves so that we can have discussion and develop a distinctive agenda in relation to our needs, our social location, our aspirations and so on". That shouldn't be seen as "oh no no, we don't do that in this country", because, why don't we do it? It's consistent with other things that we do. Another example would be the second chamber. The Church of England has by right 26 seats in that second chamber. It's not a very powerful chamber, but it is part of the architecture of the State. Other religions don't have that representation there, but a practice has grown up over time to have some inclusion, so the chief Rabbi is a member, but this is only the second time the chief Rabbi has been a member, and we couldn't say that he's there by right, but in Britain precedent is quite important. If something happens two or three times you can be sure it will become normalized. The Catholic Church has people there. Moreover, the Catholic Church is regarded as a social partner to the State in a certain number of things, above all education. Lots of State resources, meaning lots of schools, thousands of schools which are paid for by the taxpayer, are run by the Catholic Church and so on. So, why can't Muslims have some schools? Obviously not any school would do, it has to be regulated, it has to be of appropriate standard, it must have appropriate equipment, the teachers must be qualified and so on. So just someone coming along saying "I want a Muslim school" doesn't mean they get it. There are educational criteria, there are policy allocations, resource issues, but that's the kind of inclusion that I'm talking about. Things that already are done and don't seem to cause a problem, why can't they be extended to Muslims? Now, there may be certain things that Muslims might ask for, for which we don't have a clear precedent, and those become a bit more difficult. What if some Muslims say they want *Shari'a* within the United Kingdom. There are some Muslims who say that, a small number, but there are some. Even this is not entirely unprecedented, it depends on what you mean by personal law. But at the moment, and for many decades, we've had the Church of England and the Jewish Rabbinical Court settle matters like divorce and legacy and children, parental responsibility. They can't contradict UK law, their decisions can't go against UK law, it has to be nested within UK law, but they can apply theological reasoning to arrive at judgements, which have to be consensually accepted. No one is forced to go there, if you are a Jewish person and you want to divorce, you're not forced to go to that court, you may want to just go to the ordinary civil court, but if you choose to go there and your spouse chooses to go there, the other party chooses to go there, then the decision that the court makes will be legally upheld, as long as it's not breaking any UK law. So I can see a situation where we might want to allow, as it were, Muslim courts, Imams and Alims, to preside over family disputes, by those people who voluntarily recognize the authority of that court within the UK legislation. That to me would be acceptable, more than acceptable, I think it would be reasonable.

Q. *I'm just back from Pakistan. My question is: Pakistanis in Antwerp have their networks all over the world. How do we bring in international politics? Because we were not talking in Pakistan about religion, we were talking about politics. Rather difficult international stupid politics.*

A. I'm not sure I understand what the difficulty is supposed to be. People can be dual citizens, so we don't hold that against them. The UK is one of the most liberal countries in the world in relation to dual, possibly even multiple citizenship. If you are a citizen of the UK you can be a citizen of another country without even telling anybody. Nobody asks you. If you're applying for a passport in the UK that's fine if you also possess a Pakistani passport. You're not asked to renounce previous citizenship, unlike in the US, unlike in a number of other countries. So we don't think it's a problem if people have a political life outside our country. In fact we have people in our cabinet whose political careers began outside the UK. Peter Hain, at one time he was minister for Europe. He's a South African. Patricia Hewitt who is the minister for health, she comes from New Zealand.

Paul Bo-Tang, who is not in the current government but was in the previous government, has a Ghanaian parent. So if somebody for instance is active in British politics and is at the same time active in Pakistani politics, there isn't a problem. I mean it may be that some people may choose not to vote for that person, but that's just a democratic solution. There is no problem of legality. I give you one example: a group in the country who, just like in the US, are most committed to the welfare of a state other than the UK or the US, are Jewish people in relation to Israel. Israel says that all Jewish people, wherever they live, Belgium, Britain, belong to the Jewish state, they have a home in the Jewish state. No one in the UK says "oh, that's not right, they are cutting across our sovereignty", so I don't understand what the problem is. Everybody knows that many ethnic groups in the US can be very actively involved in homeland political issues, especially to do with liberation and so on. It's not just a nice idea, it works.

Q. I've been following your interesting talk very well, and I was trying to situate this opposition between multiculturalism and secularism at a European level. Multiculturalism, of course, is something which the European Union has in its own origins. It is not "we, the people", like the US, it is "the peoples of Europe", which are coming together. So certainly Europe has multiculturalism as a paradigm, and that's a favourable point. Which also means that it may be easier, – it is not, I think, but it may be easier – to welcome immigrants from other Nation-States, because Nation-States no longer exist in Europe, whereas the US is still a Nation-State with nationality, which is applauded when you are becoming a US national, which is not the case in Italy, the UK, perhaps in France, but not in Belgium. So we are clearly going toward a Citizen-State. A Citizen-State assembled around the same democratic values as is specified in Article 6 of the European treaty: "democracy, the rule of law, respect for human rights". Respect for human rights also includes the freedom of religion, but that doesn't mean that you are against secularism, of course. And that's my second point. Because among these common values, religion is not included. We have had a discussion for the drafting of the European constitution, about whether God should be in the constitution. I was not in favour of that, but anyway, we did have the discussion on having God or Allah or whatever you would like, in the constitution. So in the end it is not part of the common values of Europe, it is not considered to be part of the common values, but instead secularism is part of the European Union. All this to say that we are very ambiguous also in Europe, apart from Article 13 on discrimination, which can help the UK as it can help other countries, but that's against discrimination, it's not in favour of something. But now my own question to you, which is down to earth but which is a major question: in this opposition between secularism and multiculturalism, how do you see the position the European Union should have regarding Turkey as a bridge between Europe and the Arab world?

A. Well, firstly I think you made some assumptions about Europe and where it is going, which may or may not turn out to be true. Europe as a union of citizens, you said at one point, but at another point you said it is a union of peoples.

Q. It's in the constitution: "states and peoples".

A. I think there are quite a lot of people in Britain who would think it's bad news to be told the Nation-State no longer exists. So, anyway, I don't want to go into a discussion with you about that. The reason I raise it is that, in my analysis, I put a lot of emphasis on the variability of what secularism means in practice. As an idea it may be very simple and very transportable, you can take it all over the world, but actually what it means in practice, what secularism means for the US, is different from France, from Belgium, from Germany and so on. And then the next step of my argument was: let us be sensitive to the national context, to the institutional resources available in different national contexts, and the different challenges. So in a way I was highlighting the pragmatic desirability of national solutions, and allowing for some degree of variability. Now obviously in the EU that will be within a framework, so it won't be a completely unlimited variability, or it will be a variability within certain kinds of principle structures, but I would prefer the principal structures to be relatively loose and to allow nations to do a lot of their own interpreting and implementing. So that's how I deal with the first part of what you said.

As for the absence of the mention of religion in the European constitution and having Turkey become a part of the EU, my answer. I guess would begin with the following observation: in Britain, we have an established church, and our monarch is the Head of State and the Governor of that State. She's not a Muslim, and everybody knows she's not, and Muslims don't have a problem with it. If you said to Muslims: "would you rather have a Head of State who was an Anglican Christian or an atheist?" most Muslims would say "Anglican Christian, please". So, most Muslims in Britain are not fighting against a Christian establishment. They do think they're fighting against something, because besides kinds of discrimination and so on, they think there is a political culture which frowns upon public religion, which frowns upon religion in politics, and because they want to give Muslim identity – at least for the time being, the future might be different – a certain centrality and primacy as a community, as a people within the UK. They feel they're backing against those who would exclude religious identity. So they don't consider that their primary opponents are Christian aggrandizers, but rather religion belittlers. So then, on the question about whether we should have Christianity mentioned in some kind of preamble to the European constitution, opinion is split. Some people say "well of course, we don't want to be part of a godless Europe, so let them mention Christianity, as long as it's not exclusive", but then other people can see that for a lot of people the only reason for mentioning Christianity is so that it can be exclusive, because Christianity then is a codeword for non-Muslim, and a codeword for keeping Turkey out, so I would say that most Muslims in Britain would be keen on Turkey becoming part of the EU, and as you know, our government is as well. It's the one thing that the government and the Muslims agree on, one of the few remaining things at the moment. But there are other Muslims, including friends and colleagues of mine and so on, who are very much against Turkey joining the EU, but perhaps for the opposite reasons that are mainly circulating, because they want to see an Islamic renaissance, and they want an Islamic federation of countries, and they don't want Turkey to be pulled away from a potential Islamic future. So they say "no, Turkey should stay out of Europe until there is another federation they can join, which will not be a European one". That's not my view. I'm very keen on Turkey becoming a member, for a number of reasons, but the most pertinent of which are because I think it will help Europeans understand that we don't live in an exclusively Christian continent. We don't have an exclusively Christian history. I'm pretty confident, from the academic work that I'm seeing in Britain, that the way European history will be taught, say in 25 years' time, will be quite different from the way it has been taught. The Muslim element of European history will, at least I would say in the curricula of British universities and schools, definitely be mentioned. It's impossible really to talk about the fact that Muslims ruled several parts of Spain for 700 years, it's very difficult to write about certain changes in Christian theology in the late medieval period, if you aren't allowed to read Arabic texts and Arabic philosophers. The Greek and Roman texts that came into Europe, actually are sometimes in Arabic, and were then translated back into Latin from Arabic. So when we look at Spain, Sicily, and then of course more recent history to do with the Ottomans and South East Europe and so on, the idea that this is a Christian continent will look like such an oversimplification. I'm kind of confident about that, but on the other hand, the presence of Turkey as a full member of the European Union of course will have a tremendous impact in broadening people's understanding of what is Europe. If we did say to Turkey that it can't join, you know, if we collectively say to Turkey "no sorry, you're just not the right kind of country for us to join", and really whether we say it explicitly or implicitly, it is because we're a Christian federation of countries and you're Muslims, or you're a majority of Muslims, I think it will send a very bad signal to Muslims in Europe, because in a way it's saying to them "you can't be fully European". That's a very bad thing to say to a growing population on the continent. Muslims now are about 5% of Western Europe, of what you might call the EU 15 without the recent accession states, but in a generation's time there will be 10%. They will be very significant minorities in most of the large cities in Western Europe, such as Brussels, London, Paris and so on. To say to such a population "you can't be fully European because you're Muslim" seems to me the most blind, divisive policy to follow. We should be doing exactly the opposite: we should be saying to as many Muslims as we possibly can "you are European, you can be fully European with full equal membership and status". That is what we want, that is how we can achieve something together. So while I would like Turkey in for other reasons, one self-interested reason is that I think the way in which we may end up saying "no" to Turkey will have very serious long-term consequences inside Europe, let alone for relations with our neighbouring countries.

ISLAM, MUSLIMS AND THE WEST: RELIGION AND SECULARISM FROM POLARIZATION TO NEGOTIATION

Nasr Abu Zayd

Introduction

Since the French president announced on December 16, 2003 the necessity to introduce a new law in order to prohibit religious symbols, such as the Jewish yarmulke, the big crosses and the female Muslim headscarf, *hijâb*, to be shown in the national French schools, the reaction generated all over the Muslim World, especially in the Arab World, presents the model of the polemic controversy/dispute/debate/ discussion that has been overshadowing the relationship between the Muslim World and the Western World since the late eighteenth and the beginning of the nineteenth centuries. The issue at steak here, from the French view, is the issue of protecting the secular basis of the French society against possible threat of disintegration if the religious symbols are shown in public schools. Religious symbols in the shared public sphere of schools would identify pupils according to their religious affiliation, thus causing a serious threat to their national identity as French citizens. In order to safeguard the national French identity and to enhance the process of integration religious symbols should be prohibited from being shown in public schools.

For the Muslim World, as represented by the ʿulama, in reaction to the French presidents' announcement, *hijâb* is, unlike crosses or yarmulke, not a religious symbol; it is rather an obligatory religious requirement ordained by God and his Prophet. If a Muslim woman fails to wear the *hijâb*, she is considered a sinner and disobedient to the divine demand, and punishment in the life-after will be inflicted on her. Preventing Muslim girls by law from wearing the *hijâb* thus represents a Western enmity against Islam and discrimination against Muslims. Following all the articles published in Arabic newspapers dealing with the subject and watching some of the TV programs discussing the issue on some Arab satellites one can easily get the impression that the French move presents a severe threat to the identity of Muslims, not only in France but in the whole Muslim World and to the entire Muslim Nation, *umma*, as well.

The rector of al-Azhar in Egypt, the oldest and most influential Muslim institution in the Sunni World, tried to take a seemingly moderate position after a meeting with the French minister of interior. In the press conference following the meeting the rector of al-Azhar gave his statement: first, he declared that Islam is based on justice, which means rights are to be given to the appropriate persons, groups, or nations etc. Secondly, he explicitly pronounced the fact that the *hijâb* is a religious obligation for every Muslim woman who will be judged if she fails to perform such an obligation. Thirdly, he pronounced the right of every state to make its own laws in accordance with its own political ideology and the duty of the Muslim citizens of that State is to obey the law. Muslim women in France should, therefore, obey the French law concerning the prohibition of wearing *hijâb* in public schools. This permission is based on the principle of 'necessity' as deduced from the *Qur'ân* (ch. 2, v. 173). By such a way rights are given to all.

The *shaykh*, whose official title is the 'grand imam', became a victim of his moderate position, giving the French State its right to organize its society in one hand, and giving French Muslim women a way out by applying the principle of 'necessity' to their situation. The majority of the *'ulama* in the Arab World explicitly condemned the *sheikh*'s opinion, some went even further and declared the apostasy of the grand imam.

If the issue at stake for the French authority is to safeguard the secular nature of the state, the issue at stake for Muslims is, first, to protect the Islamic identity of the French Muslim citizens, and, secondly and more essentially, is to defend Islam against secularism, which happened to be seen as anti-religion ideology.

The French secular ideology, according to the most dominant and deeply established Muslim perspective, emerged initially as a protest against the Church's oppression of reason, rationality, scientific progress, and Enlightenment, but it gradually developed an anti-religion ideology. Secularism is, therefore, a Western European phenomenon with which Islam has nothing to do. If Christianity is basically making clear distinction between Cesar and God, preserving for each his own rights, so Muslims would argue, the distinction does not exist in Islam, where both politics and religiosity are one and the same. This view was expressed in the context of the *hjiâb* dispute in *al-Jazîra* TV channel, known as the Arabic CNN, in a program named 'The Opposite Direction' (*al-ittijâh al-mu`âkis*) broadcasted on January 6th, 2004. One of the two guests was a cleric from the above-mentioned al-Azhar institute of Egypt; he presented the orthodox Islamic anti-secular position. The second guest was Muhammad Arkoun, an Emeritus professor at the Sorbonne, who presented the Islamic liberal view. The debate and dispute between the two guests extended beyond the specific issue of *hijâb* into the problem of Islam and modernity. Arkoun defended modernity and secularism, thus justifying the French political decision as by no means an anti-Islamic. His opponent insisted that it was part of the long history of the Western enmity against Islam and Muslims. He went further in emphasizing his argument by counting the Catholic and the Protestant missionary institutions active in different parts of the Muslim World whose aim is the divert Muslims from their faith. He counted the number of missionary books, including the Bible, they freely distribute, the numbers of radio and TV stations they own as well as the numbers of the audio and videotapes they produce etc.

Modernity, according to the cleric, is a catastrophe to Islam. In his view secularism was a battle against the Church; it was a medicine invented to cure a disease that Islam never suffered. But people like Arkoun, the cleric explained, tries to import the disease, the conflict between the Church and the civil society, into the Muslim World in order to introduce secularism as a cure. When Arkoun made reference to Islamic Philosophy, especially to the philosopher Ibn Rushd – known as Averroes in the West – to prove the openness toward the others in the Islamic heritage the cleric strongly protested against associating the name of a Muslim philosopher with modernism and secularism. However, he apologetically denied that he was propagating a conflict or a clash of civilizations or cultures, quoting the *Qur'ân* where it is mentioned that God created people in different nations and tribes in order to recognize and know each other (chap. 49:13). He also quotes the *Qur'ân* where it is mentioned that it one of God's divine signs that humans are created in different skin-colors speaking different languages (ch. 30:22) It was, and still is, according to the cleric view, the West who invaded the Muslim land, thus, exploiting its economic resources and contaminating its culture, thus causing a paradigm of conflict.

Within the broadcasting which allowed viewers to participate by raising questions or by comments the channel opened an electronic vote on the question whether secularism is anti-religion or not. The result of the poll was that 89% of the voters, counted as 983,002900, believe that secularism is anti-religion while only 11% found it not.[2]

---

[2] See the website:
http://www.aljazeera.net/programs/op_direction/articles/2004/1/1-10-2.htm

Now the question is, why the Muslim World in general and the Arab World in particular, became so entrapped in discussing the issue of *hjiâb* as if it were the backbone of Islamic identity for females? On the other hand, one is tempted to question as well the French secularism, what kind of danger or threat quite a number of head-covered girls present to the legacy of the French secular republic? It is even more tempting to raise the dilemma of the version of secularism that despises and disrespects the world of symbols, whether religious, cultural or even ethnic. Why it is so joyful and celebrated in arts, literature, dresses and food while it is so intolerable in the domain of religion? Such questions are essential questions to be talked if we have to reach a point of mutual understanding, a point of meeting in between two fundamentalisms: secular fundamentalism and religious fundamentalism.

The dilemma of polarization – secularism vs. religion – is not new; it is, for Muslims at least, the continuation of the imperial Europe manipulating its inventions, including Enlightenment, rationalism, democracy and human rights, to dominate the non-European world and get hold of its economic resources? This polemic dispute started as early as the beginning of the nineteenth century?

I have intentionally inserted 'Muslims' in the title of the paper in order to clarify a long and well-established confusion in the Western discourse as well as in modern Islamic discourse. This confusion can be explained in terms of entrapping and being entrapped. If by analyzing the cause of this ailment, we might be in a position to suggest a negotiation strategy to tackle the problem.

Islam and Christianity: Different Historical Paradigms

If compared with the Christian experience, two different historical facts have to be attended. First point is the different historical context, while Christianity was born in an already established empire Islam was born in a tribal context. Christianity has to wait till the fourth century before it became the official religion of the Roman Empire. Islam, on the other hand, developed immediately to establish its unique independent community that gradually was able to build up its political and military power, first, in Hijaz from which its power was spread all over Arabia, and soon after started to invade the boundaries of the great empires of the world at that time *i.e.*, the Roman and the Persian. From this specific historical context, we can explain the powerful relation between Islam and politics compared to the circumstantial relation in Christianity. Whether or not this can provide satisfactory explanation for the separation between religion and politics in Christianity or not is another issue of investigation.

The politicization of Islam started when the tribe of the Prophet Mohammed, Quraysh, tried to make religion a piece of tribal property by calming that his successor should come from the same tribe. Islam was originally a community religion, but it turned with very little difficulty to be a state/empire religion, centred particularly on the tribe of Prophet Mohammed. Right after the announcement of the Prophet's death, a heated debate took place between the people of Mecca, the Muhajirîn or immigrants, and the people of Medina, the Ansâr or supporters of the Prophet, about the 'successor-ship' issue. A serious conflict arose between the two groups that was about to turn to violence, but an agreement was reached by choosing the oldest person Abû-Bakr, who happened to be the Prophet's father in law, as the first Caliph. Nevertheless, the issue of 'Caliphate' turned to be a major political issue especially during the era of civil war known as 'fitnah'.

After the assassination of the third caliph, the first civil war in Islamic history began between the fourth caliph and other companions of the Prophet, including his wife ᶜAisha. This created three political parties with three different opinions concerning this issue. One group of Muslims, the Shiʿîs, which proved to be a minority, believed that the Prophet had in fact designated his successor, and that was his son-in-law and cousin, Alî. Another group which formed the majority of Muslims, the Sunnis, took the view that the Prophet had deliberately left the question of his succession open, leaving it to the community to decide who would be the most competent person to assume its leadership, but they emphasized that Caliphate should be only confined to the Meccan aristocracy (*Quraish*), the Prophet's tribe. The third major political trend in early Islam was the rejection of both the Sunni and the Shiʿîs positions, and its followers came to be appropriately known as the *Khawârij* (plural of Kharijî, meaning an outsider.) Allied to their uncompromising attachment to the *Qur'ân* was a democratic temper insisting on the right of all Muslims, irrespective of their tribal, racial and class distinction, to elect or dispose, or to be elected as, rulers.[3] As the *Khawârij* started to support their political position by quoting

---

[3] See, Hamid Enayat, *Modern Islamic Political thought*, The Macmillan Press LTD, London, 1982, pp. 4–7.

some verses of the *Qur'ân*, Islamic theology started to emerge and the *Qur'ân*, or rather its interpretation and counter-interpretation, became to be at the heart of it.

Another feature of distinction between the Christian historical experience and that of Islam has to do with the theological/intellectual development. Christianity first had Catholicism that in some senses constituted a comprehensive or holistic social order; and then the Reformation and Protestantism, which, of course, was one of several inputs into the modernization process in Europe over past centuries. Islamic development was, in a way, the exact opposite. Islamic culture began with the rational school of interpretation, which tried to understand the Text in its socio-cultural context and to reinterpret it accordingly, in order to open up the meaning of the Text, or to render it capable of being opened up as history progressed. This process began in the second Islamic century, the eighth century by European reckoning. But then, the traditional understanding, the 'Orthodox', dominated the whole of the Islamic world.

The Modernity Dilemma

Modernity, as it is well known, was introduced to the Muslim World in the context of being dominated by the European colonial power. By the end of nineteenth century, the British had successfully colonized much of India. The French, under Napoleon Bonaparte, occupied Egypt in 1798. France then went into Algeria in 1830; occupied Tunisia in 1881, and Britain marched into Egypt in 1882. There were many other excursions as the West's program of the colonization unfolded throughout the Muslim World.

Within the military power there was an intellectual weapon advocating the necessity of neglecting and abandoning Islam, if this part of the world was to make any progress toward catching with modernity. It is enough to mention the French philosopher Ernest Renan (1832-1892), and the French politician and historian Gabriel Hanotaux (1853-1944)[4], who served as Minister of Foreign Affairs during 1894 and 1898. Renan posited the absolute incompatibility between Islam and both

---

[4] A statesman, diplomat, and historian who directed a major French colonial expansion in Africa and who championed a Franco-Russian alliance that proved important in the events leading to World War I. As a French nationalist he was committed to policies of colonial expansion. During his ministry, French domination was established in French West Africa, Madagascar, and Tunisia; inroads were made in Algeria.

sciences and philosophy. Whatever is labelled Islamic science or Islamic philosophy is, according to Renan in his doctoral thesis, *Averroès et l'Averroïsme* (1852; 'Averroës and Averroism'), mere translation from the Greek. Islam, like all religious dogmas built on revelation, is hostile to reason and freethinking.[5] Hanotaux too held Islam responsible for the backwardness of the Muslim world. His allegation was based on the theological difference between Islam and Christianity. According to him the dogma of incarnation in Christianity has its consequence in building a bridge between man and God, thus freeing man from any dogma of determinism. Islamic pure monotheism, *tawhîd*, on the other hand, has created non-bridged distance between man and God, leaving no space for human free well. By such theological reason Hanotoux explained the political despotism characterizing the Muslim World.[6]

Against these severe allegations against Islam, both Jamâl al-Dîn al-Afghânî (1839-1897) and Mohammad Abduh (1848-1905) responded defensively, relating the backwardness of Muslims not to Islam *per se*, but to the contemporary Muslims' misunderstanding of Islam. They both argue, if Islam is understood properly and explained correctly, as was the case in the golden age of Islamic civilisation, Muslims would not have been easily defeated, and dominated by European power.

The basic question that confronted the early modern Muslim reformers was whether Islam is compatible with modernity or not. How could a faithful Muslim live in a modern socio-political environment, without losing her/his identity as a Muslim? Does Islam accommodate science and philosophy? Second came the question of the compatibility or otherwise of the divine law (*shari'a*) that constitutes traditional society, and the positive law that constitutes the modern Nation-State. Were modern political institutions such as democracy, elections, and parliament accepted by Islam, and could they replace the traditional institutions of *shûrâ*, consultation, and the authority of the elite `ulama (*ahl al-hall wa al-'aqd*)?

Al-Afghânî was heavily occupied of fighting against the imperial power politically and intellectually, thus combining agitate activism with intellectual maneuver all over the Muslim World, in India, Iran, Egypt and Turkey. "He supported movements working for constitutional liberties and fought for liberation from foreign control (Egypt, Persia).

---

[5] See, Ahmad Amân, Min *Zu`ma' al-Islâh* (Some Pioneers of Reformation,) The Egyptian National Books' Organization, Cairo, reprint 1996, 2nd. vol., pp. 40–48.

[6] See the translation of Hanotaux' article into Arabic and Muhammad `Abduh's response in *al-A'mal al-Kamilah*, (the Complete Works), ed. Muhammad 'Amarah, Beirut 1972-1974, v. 5, p. 201f.

He attacked Muslim rulers who opposed reform or did not show enough resistance to European encroachments. He even envisaged the possibility of political assassination. His ultimate object was to unite Muslim states (including Shi`î Persia) into a single Caliphate, able to repulse European interference and recreate the glory of Islam. The pan-Islamic idea was the great passion of his life. He remained unmarried, survived with the absolute minimum in the way of food and clothing and took no stimulants other than tea and tobacco."[7]

Abduh, on the other hand, concentrated his activity in the arena of thought, especially after he was exiled because of his participation in `Urabî's affair which ended with the British occupation of Egypt in 1882. Influenced heavily by Afghânî, Abduh adopted a synthesis of classical rationalism, and modern socio-political awareness. This made it possible for him to re-examine the basic sources of Islamic knowledge, the *Qur'ân* and the *Sunna* (the Tradition of the prophet,) as well as the structure of Islamic theology, thus, preparing the ground for what to be known as the islâh, reformation, movement.

The question of Islam and modern knowledge, which was fundamental to Abduh's writings, led him to re-examine Islamic heritage by reopening the 'door of *ijtihâd*' (free reasonable reflection) in all aspects of social and intellectual life. As religion is an essential part of human existence, he argued that the only avenue through which to launch real reform was through a reform of Islamic thought. He was deeply influenced by Jamâl al-Dîn al-Afghânî (1839-1897) who had brought to Egypt the idea of a new, modern interpretation of Islam.

The movement of reformation first advocated by Afghânî and Abdu represents to us nowadays a process of negotiating tradition as well as negotiating the challenge of the West. Such a movement is still alive and progressing, though unnoticed in the Western public sphere. There is no move from the Western side to reconsider its modernizing values as absolute; these values are the norms to be followed, peacefully or by enforcement, by all the nations on earth.

Even with the case of Turkey, where another response to the European challenge is adopted since 1924, *i.e.*, the secular separation between the state and religion, turkey is not yet accepted to join the Western club, the European Union. It worth noting that when the Kemalist movement abolished the caliphate under the pressure the Western power after the World war one, the reaction in the Islamic world was extremely

---

[7] I. Goldziher and J. Jomier's article, *The Encyclopedia of Islam*, 2nd ed., Brill, Leiden, vol. 11, pp. 416–417.

emotional. In my opinion, the united response is explained by the fact the whole Islamic world felt it had been left naked by being stripped off this symbolic caliphate – it was already symbolic at that time. Only one year before it was abolished, the Kemalists very wisely separated caliphate and sultanate, which was a radical secular decision. This decision was warmly welcomed – at least in Egypt. One reason was the traditional distinction between political and religious authorities, a distinction that almost unrealized because of the stereotype image of Islam in the West. Another reason, I think, was that the probably Egyptians thought that the caliph would now be the Caliph of all Muslims, not the political leader of the Turks. They believed that the authentic Islamic system was not at all the same thing as the political authority of the Turks, although the Ottoman authority had come to symbolize it. So the reaction was very positive. But the total abolition of caliphate left the whole Islamic world feeling it had been stripped naked. And it is easy to understand the subsequent chain of events: the decision to end the system was taken in 1924, and a new phase of intellectual reaction to the challenge against Islam started.

Re-politicization

Nevertheless, one of Abdu's disciples `Alî `Abd al-Râziq, a prominent Azhar cleric, defended the abolition of the Caliphate and argued for the separation of religion and state on grounds internal to the traditional Qur'ânic, prophetic, and legal Islamic discourses and narratives. His book, Islam and the Principles of Political Authority Al-Islâm wa Usûl 'l-Hukm, (Cairo 1925), turned, at the time, into a major literary-religious scandal in both the Arab and Muslim Worlds leading to the author's expulsion from al-Azhar. His central argument was that "the Caliphate had no basis either in the Qur'ân, nor the Tradition, or the consensus. To prove each part of this argument, he dealt in some details with the major pieces of evidence which are normally drawn from these three sources in establishing the 'obligatory' of the Caliphate. He rightly said that the Qur'ân nowhere makes any mention of the Caliphate in the specific sense of the political institution we know in history. (...) Nor can any convincing proof be extracted from the sayings attributed to the prophet. ... ... To dispose of consensus as the last, conceivable sanction, `Abd 'l-Râziq argued that, judging from concrete historical instances, consensus, whether in the sense of the agreement of the

Prophet's Companions and their followers, or that of the *'Ulamâ'* of the entire Muslim community, has never played any role in installing the Caliphs."[8]

If the position of 'Alî 'Abd al-Raziq presents continuation of the reformist trend of thought, the abolishment of caliphate created an opposite reaction led to a rather radical Islamic movement, *i.e.*, the Muslim Brotherhood, *Al-Ikhwân al-Muslimûn*, founded in Egypt in 1928 by Hasan al-Bannâ. It was inspired by the thought of Muhammad Rashîd Rida, a disciple and co-editor of the *Tafsîr al-Manâr* with Mohammad Abduh, who was involved in the dispute against *Abd al-Raziq*; he emphasised the religious necessity, *wujûb*, of Caliphate to Muslims to the extent he considered the Muslim World without it as returning back to paganism, *Jahiliyya*.[9] Secondly, contrary to his professor Abduh, who mostly adopted the rationalized Islamic trend of thought as we mentioned above, Rida distinguished himself as follower of the Hanbalî school as was developed by both *Ibn Taimiyya* and *Ibn al-Qayyim*.[10] It was Muslim Brotherhood Society the organization from which all the radical islamist groups emerged.

As a reactionary movement, the re-establishment of Caliphate was at the top of Muslim Brothers' agenda. In other words, it was the making of God's word kingdom; the *Qur'ân* is its constitution, and *jihad* is the means to make it true. Al-Banna simplified the Wahabi dogma and made it stricter in order to function as the ideological basis of a powerful popular movement.

- Islam is an 'order', *nizâm*, without equal, because it is revealed by God, which has a vocation to organize all aspects of human life; it is dogma and worship, fatherland and nationality, religion and state, spirituality and action, *Qur'ân* and sword. This order is valid for all men of all time and all countries.
- Muslims should return back to the faith of the 'devout ancestors', al-salaf, of the Community, Ummah, which is devoid of non-*Qur'ân*ic influences brought about in theology and philosophy which are impregnated with the Greek spirit, which is foreign to primitive Islam, and whose speculations had provoked in the past, and have encouraged in the present time, divisions and a sectarian spirit, which form an obstacle to the necessary unity of all Muslims which is indispensable

---

[8] Hamid Enayat, *ibid.*, pp. 69–79.
[9] *Ibid.*
[10] Cf. *Tafsîr al-Manâr* (Al-Manâr commentary of the *Qur'ân*), 2nd ed., Cairo, 1961, vol.1, p. 211.

in their struggle against the foreign imperialists. The believer can know God only through the description which He has given himself in the *Qur'ân* and through the words of His prophet.[11]
- Re-islamization of life in Egypt in all the fields which have been infected by Western influence, now considered to be waning; these extended from social habits, such as dress, greeting, the use of foreign languages, hours of works and rest, the calendar, recreation, etc., to the educational, legal and political institutions, not to mention the fields of ideas and sentiment. Matters relating to the family and to the position of women were not neglected. One of the main points in Ikhwan's program was the abolition of the Egyptian legal codes based on European codes, and the creation of a legislation based on *shari'a*.[12]
- This should be considered a preparatory step towards the final goal, which is to restore a single state that will embrace all the Muslim people and would have at its head a caliph.

Most of the scholarship concerned with fundamentalism focus only on the doctrines expressed by the militant extremists like *Jihad*, Jama'at Islâmyyha, Hizb Allah, Al-Takfîr wa Al-Hijrah etc., excluding other fundamentalist movement, namely Muslim Brotherhood, on ground that it is theologically 'moderate ', politically against 'violence' and intellectually 'rational'. If this was the case at the beginning phase of this movement, the second quarter of this century, it has not been the same since the end of the forties. Now, the distinction between 'moderate' and 'extreme' Islamists is of a degree not of a kind; they are like a sound and its echo. Both adhere to the same 'Orthodox' theology turning it to an ideology against the ill-established modern civil societies in Muslim countries. The ideological basis of this fundamentalist discourse could be summarized in at least five points as follows:

---

[11] Later on, *Sayyid Qutb*, the theoretician of militant fundamentalism, elaborated this notion of the 'absolute pure spring' of knowledge, the *Qur'ân*, and made it the criterion according to which any knowledge should be judged and evaluated. According to Qutb, all philosophies, social sciences and political systems of the world are nothing but different modes of paganism, *jahiliyyah*, where sovereignty is in the hand of man instead of God *Cf. Maâlim fi al-Tarîq* (Marks on the Road), Dar al-Shurûq, Cairo, 1982, pp. 14–15, 142–148.

[12] During their collision with Sadat's regime (1970-1981) in the early seventies, they could introduce an amendment to the second article of the Egyptian constitution to be "the principles of shari'a are the main source (instead of 'one of the sources') of legislation."

- An identification of human 'thought' and 'religion' and an elimination of the distance between 'subject' and 'object.'
- An explanation of all phenomena by reducing them to single first principle or a single cause. This explanation includes all scientific as well as social phenomena.
- A reliance on the tyranny of either 'the past' or 'tradition,' and this by converting secondary traditional texts into primary ones, which are endowed with sanctity that in many instances is scarcely less than that of the primary text, the *Qur'ân*.
- An absolute mental certainty and intellectual decisiveness that refuses to brook any disagreement at all, except in negligible details, which in any event have no basis or principles, or 'fundamentals' for them.
- Avoidance or ignorance of the historical dimension which manifests itself in weeping over the wonderful past embodied in the golden age of the Caliph Haroun al-Rashid or the caliphate of the Ottoman Empire.[13]

Moderate discourse, for example, insists on substituting *sharî`a* for democracy, whereas it has been considered in the reforming discourse as the ground for justifying and establishing democracy. Democracy in the eyes of the new Islamic movements is a western invention that allows people absolute free choice, while an islamic system is the recognition of sharî`a and its implementation as the only source of legislation. The choice of the public has, therefore, to be limited to their representatives who would guard it.

Another yet different example is the Iranian case. The ayatollah in their moment of victory in 1979 did not proceed to restore the Islamic caliphate nor did they erect an Imamate or vice-Imamate. They proceeded to establish a republic for the first time in Iran's long history, a republic with popular election, a constituent assembly, a parliament, a president, a council of ministers, political factions, a constitution, a kind of supreme court and so on.[14] This leads us to uncover the similarity between the secular State of Turkey and the Islamic Republic of Iran. In both instances, as well as in most of the Muslim countries, secularization of life has been an ongoing process regardless of the high voices of radical Islamism. The victory of the reformists against traditionalists in

---

[13] *Cf.* Nasr Abu-Zaid, *Naqd al-Khitâb al-Dînî*, Critique of Islamic Discourse, 3rd ed., Madbouly, Cairo, 1995, pp.67–68.

[14] Sadik. J. al-Azm, *Is Islam Secularizable?*, unpublished paper presented at the Conference "Challenging Fundamentalism: Questioning Political and scholarly Simplification", Kuala Lumpur, Malaysia, 26–27 April, 1996.

Iran was very visible and very promising until Mr. Bush classified Iran among the evil-axe States.

Negotiation or Confrontation

How much change could be noticed now in the relationship between the West and the Muslim world? How much pressure is still practiced against the Muslim world to protect the economic and political interest of the West? How many unjust political regimes were supported by the political West against the will of the people? How much political manipulation is played against Muslims by presenting Islam as the substitute enemy of the West after the falling apart of the Soviet Union? If the conflict of civilizations is unavoidable, why should Muslims accept the values of a civilization they have to destroy? It is true that the world has become a small village, but in this very small village the poor living in the South are getting poorer, while the rich of the North are getting richer. Modernity, Human Rights, democracy are only for the privileged, for the under privileged there is nothing but to cry for justice. In this cry, not in Islam itself, sometimes violent, resides the question of modernity and all its relevance.

SCIENCE AND RELIGION, AN UNEASY RELATIONSHIP IN THE HISTORY OF JUDEO-CHRISTIAN-MUSLIM HERITAGE

Sadik J. al-Azm

Islam's Satanic Tragedy, as Described in Sadik al-Azm's Exegesis: Introduction by Jean-pierre Rondas

Behind the *Satanic Verses* lurks not just the novelist Salman Rushdie, but indeed, as the phrase literally indicates, the devil himself. That his verses had disappeared (or – *horribile dictu* – been cancelled) from Sura 53 'The Star' of the *Qur'ân* does not take away from the fact that they had been 'there'. Muhammad was their mental receiver and scribe, unaware of their being inspired by the devil and not, as usual, by Gibreel. Their actual absence only bears witness to their one-time presence. In this way, Iblis has had his negative share in the editing of the *Qur'ân*.

Salman Rushdie was not the first Islamic-secularized intellectual to have written about, and elaborated on, the status of the Islamic devil and his verses. The Syrian philosopher and philologist Sadik al-Azm had done so some two decades before Rushdie, in a remarkable fifty-page essay called *The Devil's Tragedy*. Delivered by the author before the American Cultural Circle of Beirut on December 10, 1965, and published in a short version in a cultural magazine in 1966, it was the beginning of a long series of publications in which al-Azm tried his hand at a 20th century continuation of the kind of *Qur'ân*ic hermeneutics which flourished in the Middle Ages.

When I first read this text (in a Dutch collection of his essays) I could not help comparing it with that other famous collection of essays on the devil, by the Christian philosopher Leszek Kolakowski in his *Conversations with the Devil* of 1961. One of the significant parallels is that Christian preoccupations with the Evil One are very much related to their Islamic counterparts. The one conspicuous difference in style and approach is that, whereas Kolakowski was able to base his ironic and diabolic impersonations on an ingrained western exegetical tradition, al-Azm had to allow for a much more literally-minded readership to which he had to make very clear in what kind of register he wants to reason and write.

What is this tragedy the devil had been subject to? God had ordered Iblis to prostrate himself at His creature, man – a gesture which the selfsame God had always forbidden to his angels and djinns. This creates a tragic inner conflict in the devil's soul: shall he obey God's contingent order ('kneel before man') or rather what he interprets as God's transcendent will ('never kneel before a created being')? Some medieval interpreters (interpreted, on their turn, by Sadik al-Azm) explain the tragedy in that the devil had been outwitted by God's cunning, which the devil thought he was able to counter by having recourse to God's own law. The result was that he posed as God's competitor by willing exactly what God 'really' wanted, in being 'true to God'. In this way, the cunning Godhead becomes 'good' and the true servant 'evil'. Some say that in the same way, God wanted to create the semblance of a dualism in which the good God and the evil Devil are contenders – just because this is what humans want. In the end, what people really understand is antagonism, strife, and dualism. This was the division of labour which God had decided between himself and the 'Devil'. That is why He had misled his Fallen Angel by means of an impossible order (namely to prostrate himself at a creature).

Sadik al-Azm collected his material not only from the usual fragments and scraps scattered in the *Qur'ân*, but also from the commentaries written by the *Qur'ân*'s medieval interpreters who explain this semblance of a dualism (a seeming opposition between good and evil) as the ultimate sign of God's unicity and uniqueness – even the devil's refusal to obey pays homage to this monotheism. This was exactly what al-Azm wanted to continue and to reintroduce: a kind of *Qur'ân*ic hermeneutics, which considers the *Qur'ân*ic stories (and their continuations) as human mythological stories which have to be decoded by exegesis, just as the Greek story of Antigone or the biblical story in the Book of Job have to be continuously interpreted. It is exactly such decoding which in the last resort exposes all kinds of dualism as the sham they are – which he demonstrated in the light of the Devil's story. One of the most dangerous kinds of dualism is in fact the literality of the pious who read these stories literally and indeed 'faithfully'.

At a very early stage in his career, al-Azm raised the problem of how, as a 20th century intellectual, and with the state of knowledge that we have at a given moment, a reasonable man should deal with Holy Scriptures. With this 'western' style of interpretation based on his eastern predecessors, he took up position against the literal reading of Holy scriptures in general, and of the *Qur'ân* specifically. When he published a shortened version of his five-part essay in 1966, the text was more or less considered as the by-product of the normal activities of a young professor.

Only when the full version was published in his collection of essays on *Scientific Culture and the Poverty of Religious Thought* of 1969, did the essay provoke political, religious, and ideological reactions. The local mufti pronounced a *fatwa* against al-Azm, and the author was indicted with apostasy. He was brought before court, and since apostasy is considered to be a criminal and even a capital offence, he seriously ran the risk of being sentenced to death. Twenty years before the Rushdie case (against an author who used the same *Qur'ân*ic and exegetical sources as al-Azm did before) the *fatwa* pronounced against Sadik al-Azm caused an enormous uproar in academic and religious circles in the Middle East.

At this point, a rough sketch of Sadik al-Azm's cultural and social background might be in place. The class he belongs to has always found itself in two areas of tension: one tension between different political, religious and ethnical allegiances; and another between religious and civic regulations – in fact the subjects to which Sadik al-Azm devoted his professional life. Syrian by birth and educated in Lebanon, he is in fact of 'Ottoman' and Turkish descent. His family belonged to the Ottoman ruling class in Damascus; its power dates back to the 17th and 18th centuries – witness the famous al-Azm palace next to the Damascus bazaar. Just before the first World War, the family was involved in an ambitious Ottoman railway construction project that planned to connect Istanbul with Medina. The hub of the system was to be Damascus, the oldest of the Empire's big cities.

This projected network of railway lines puts a different light on what a modernized, secularized and 'poly-ethnic' Ottoman Empire could have been like, before the first World War utterly dismantled it and made its remaining components an easy prey to European colonialism under the guise of different mandates. As it was, only the Empire's old Turkish heartland had been really secularized by the agency of Kemalist nationalism, which preserved the country from Western occupation. The price paid for this secularisation was the idea and practice of Ottoman multiculturalism itself. The 'Turkish' family al-Azm continued to stay in Damascus, now the capital of the new Syrian state under French mandate. A member of the family, Khalid bey al-Azm, even became prime minister. The family's political influence lasted until 1963, when the new pan-Arabic nationalist Baath party seized power.

From 1953 until 1957, the young Syrian Sadik al-Azm studied at the Lebanese American University of Beirut. He wrote his doctoral thesis on the French philosopher Henri Bergson at the University of Yale, and then worked for two years at the university of Damascus. In 1967, he published his study on Immanuel Kant's theory of time and on the Kantian antinomies. The year before, 1966, saw the publication of his essay on the Devil's tragedy. Only in 1969 was he summoned to appear in court for blasphemy and apostasy.

What had happened between 1966 and 1969? Was it just the difference between a shorter and a longer version of the same text of which everybody knew what it implied? The answer is another fatidical date. In the median point between those years lies 1967, the year of the overwhelming Arabic defeat at the hands of the Israelis in the Six Day's War. Sadik al-Azm responded immediately with two important publications: *Self-criticism after the Defeat* (1968), and *Critique of Religious Thought* (1969), a collection of essays on the obscurantism of Islamic traditionalism, which included the meanwhile notorious story of the Devil's tragedy.

The lawsuit took three years, from 1968 tot 1970. In a Lebanon where the liberal bourgeoisie still could make its influence felt, Sadik al-Azm was ultimately cleared of the charge of apostasy; but curiously enough, he was dismissed by his own 'western' university, the American University of Beirut, out of political correctness *avant la lettre:* the fact that there had been an apostasy case against him was already sufficient. The next seven years saw him working at the Palestinian Research Centre in Beirut, where he was in fact a free lance writer and collaborated to the *Arabic Studies Review*. From 1977 he was back at the university of Damascus, where he taught European philosophy until his retirement in 1999. Since then, he has shared his vast knowledge and sound judgement with students and researchers all over the world, specifically in Antwerp and Wassenaar; whereas his colleagues in Tübingen honoured him with the famous Leopold Lucas Prize, which he now shares with people like Karl Popper, Paul Ricoeur, and Leopold Senghor.

Immediately after the publication of Salman Rushdie's *Satanic verses* (1988), Sadik al-Azm began to document the whole discussion during the Rushdie affair, in a series of searching articles with titles as *The Tabooing Mentality: Salman Rushdie and the Truth of Literature*, or *The Importance of Being Earnest About Salman Rushdie*, or *The Satanic Verses Post Festum: the Global, the Local, the Literary*. According to al-Azm, Rushdie's novel constitutes his contribution to the enlightenment of Islam. The novel is an indication of the possibility that Islam is, indeed, secularizable. Many western intellectuals were not willing to support Rushdie, again out of an inappropriate political correctness, an attitude of which nobody has as yet been able to accuse al-Azm. In fact, al-Azm was the only Arab intellectual to have sided with Rushdie. This stance has been complicated by his at times sarcastic criticism of Edward Said's concept of orientalism, against which Said was only able to respond with holy indignation…

Sadik al Azm is a secularized Muslim, whose recurrent theme is that of the secularizability of Islam. He is continuously on the search for the hidden roots of an enlightened and humanistic train of thought in the rationalistic as well as in the mystical traditions of premodern Islamic Arabic culture. That is why, according to al-Azm, postmodernism's relativism damages the Islamic and Arabic cultures and civilisations that it pretends to defend in a multicultural way. Multiculturalism excludes western values from the Muslim experience, whereby once again Islam is locked up in its own identity. But al-Azm's analysis goes further than only this anti-relativistic stance.

Islam itself is, as it said in the Bible, 'divided against itself'. Sadik al-Azm opposes the yes-faction to the no-faction, reformation Islam against counter-reformation Islam. The historical yes-faction (which has existed as long as Islam exists) is perfectly compatible with such a modern secular paradigm. Counterreformation Islam (with the fundamentalism of the Muslim Brotherhood) pronounces a dogmatic no. According to this faction, Islam will never be compatible with modern secular paradigm. This is the impasse at which Islam has arrived nowadays.

There might be a breakthrough in this deadlock, and it is, again, Sadik al-Azm who has shown the way in which this breakthrough might be reached. There is, in fact, a historical parallel to what could happen in due time. Muslim fundamentalism (with its literalism and its violent actions) might disappear in the way that the terrorism of the Brigate Rosse and the Rote Armee Fraktion has dissolved. This historical impasse originated in the growing awareness that communism would fail. Sadik al-Azm calls this awareness, which explains the over-reactions in *action directe* style, the *reality principle*, a psycho-analytic concept which had been present in his work from his early writings on *Self-Criticism after the Defeat* from 1968 onwards.

Experiencable reality as it is manifested in history (and is still manifesting itself) has a voice. It is the voice of experience, which has enabled the West to overcome dogmatic limitations. With this liberating (Kantian) self-criticism the West has overcome a fundamentalist denial of reality, in favour of a rationality open to experience. Sadik al-Azm's criticism of Islam is a passionate plea to introduce once more this reality principle into the Islamic configuration of beliefs. In fact, he has done his fair share in trying to accomplish such a cultural revolution.

Sadik J. al-Azm's Lecture

Introduction

This paper addresses a topic involving a lot of intercultural relations, namely the on going conflicts and controversies between science and the kind of culture it generates on the one hand, and religion and the kind of culture it engenders on the other. The situation is complicated these days by still more intercultural relations – both conflictual and complimentary – involving Islam, Christianity, the East, the West and so on.

So, let me take off with the observation that it has never been easy to reconcile science and religion, autonomous reason and divine revelation in the long, rich and varied history of the Judeo-Christian-Muslim heritage and traditions. This has been most obviously and most acutely the case in the European Christian lands and cultures that saw the birth of capitalism, the rise of modernity and the explosion of the scientific revolution, all followed by a series of unending sub-scientific revolutions, continuing to this very day. These same lands and cultures were also the place where the most dramatic, decisive and consequential epistemological, historical, cultural, legal and political battles between science and religion were fought, settled and then again unsettled.

The consequences of these fights, conflicts, oppositions, settlements and unsettlements remain with us both in today's secular West as well as today's Muslim East. For an example in the West, take the strife engendered by the passionate disputes over such questions as creationism, intelligent design, embryonic stem-cell research, and the results of supposedly long-awaited medical studies conducted to scientifically test the power of prayer to cure the sick, all occurring now in some of the most scientifically and technologically advanced societies in the world and in the United States, in particular.[1]

---

[1] See, "Long Awaited Medical Study Questions to Power of Prayer", *The New York Times*, March 31, 2006. Also, *The Christian Science Monitor*, April 3 and 6, 2006

Controversies between autonomous reason and divine revelation in the history of Western thought

It was only in December 2005, that an American Federal Judge ruled that "it was unconstitutional for a Pennsylvania school district to present intelligent design as an alternative to evolution in high school biology courses because intelligent design is a religious viewpoint that advances a particular version of Christianity." This affair commanded US national attention for a while in spite of the fact that both the Supreme Court as well as the lower courts had already ruled against teaching creationism and so called creation-science in the science classes of American public schools on grounds that such doctrines violated the principle of the separation of church and state, involved supernatural explanations, and are not science in any recognizable sense of the term. In Oakland California, an advocacy group that promotes teaching evolution said that "the intelligent design advocates are expected to be much smarter in the future about concealing their religious intents", and the struggle continues.[2]

Very recently the Pope lent extra urgency to the subject, on this side of the Atlantic, by again raising contentiously in his Munich Sermon as well as in his lecture at the University of Regensburg in Bavaria, (Sept.10 & 12, 06 respectively) issues like God, man and science, the relationship of reason to faith and of faith to reason in an age of science, and the relationship of all that to other cultures, religions and traditions, including Islam. The title page of the Pope's lecture displays prominently its purpose: "Meeting with the Representatives of Science" and then proceeds to give the following title to the lecture itself: "Faith, Reason, and the University: Mémoires and Reflections." Pope Benedict's intervention speaks again of "the intrinsic necessity of a rapprochement between Biblical faith and Greek inquiry" (i.e., autonomous reason) and insists that this point is of decisive importance not only on account of its historical significance but also because "it is an event which concerns us even today."

For an example in the East, take the sharp debates and vociferous controversies raging in the Islamic world (as well as among Muslims every where else around the world) over such issues as the Islamization of modern knowledge in general and of scientific knowledge in

---

[2] See, J. Shulevitz, "When Cosmologies Collide", *New York Times Review of Books*, January 22, 2006, p. 10.

particular, all taking place right now in some of the most scientifically backward and scientifically ignorant societies on earth.[3]

What does the Islamization of knowledge mean? Does it mean, for example, putting modern scientific knowledge at the service of Islam? Or, does it mean trying to trace back the major truths discovered by modern science about the world back to the *Qur'ân* (as many have claimed and done)? Or, does it mean something a kin to the old calls for setting up a proletarian science as against the dominant bourgeois science? Or, perhaps the whole question of the Islamization of knowledge is simply incoherent? To what extent it is really a trick on the part of Muslim elites and modernizers to naturalize and acclimatize science in local Muslim communities by making it look – somehow, one way or the other, by hook or by crook – Islamic?

Here, I am on purpose emphasizing the Judeo-Christian-Muslim heritage and tradition because we rarely ever hear of a conflict of science and religion involving such other world-historical religions as Buddhism and Hinduism. This goes to show how Semitico-centric we all are in our conception of religion, where the clash of science with really three specific and highly related Middle Eastern religions imperceptibly becomes, in our discourses and debates, the clash of religion in general with modern science. I will not now go into the question why only the three major Semitic religions seem to generate a sharp conflict between science and religion, reason and faith. Does it have something to do with strict monotheism? Or, perhaps with their insistence on an absolute monopoly of the truth? Or, maybe because these religions go out of their way to affirm propositions and make claims about the world that science, reason and experience often contradict?

The most important classical rehearsal for these modern conflicts, disputes and polemics is to be found in the greatest – but usually not-so-well appreciated – controversy between autonomous reason, on the one hand, and divine revelation on the other, that occurred in the history of Western philosophical thought – broadly conceived – and I mean: first, Al-Ghazzali's bitter polemic in 11th century Baghdad against Hellenized Islamic scholastic philosophical and scientific reason as contained in his famous work: *The Incoherence of the Philosophers,* directed against such philosophers-scientists and physicians of the time as Al-Kindi,

---

[3] The best overall account of these debates in English are: (1) L. Stenberg, *The Islamization of Science: Four Muslim Positions*, University of Lund, Sweden, 1996, (2) M. Abaza, *Debates on Islam and Knowledge in Malaysia and Egypt*, Routledge Curzon, London, 2002.

Al-Farabi and Ibn-Sina (Avicenna) and their ancient Greek masters.[4] And second, Ibn Rushd's (Averroes) counter polemic and refutation in defense of that very reason, and of those very philosophers contained in his no less celebrated work *The Incoherence of the Incoherence*, all taking place in 12th century Muslim Spain.[5]

Those familiar with the case know that Al-Ghazzali, the theologian, had compiled a Syllabus or catalogue of the 20 major and most grievous errors produced by the philosophico-scientific reason of the time that conflicted with and rudely violated the Islamic orthodoxy of the moment. He denounced 17 of those errors as plain heretical innovations and condemned the remaining 3 as out-and-out apostasy, infidelity and kufr on the part of the philosopher-scientists under attack.

Among the major issues at stake in this massive and pregnant confrontation was the scientific and rational principle of natural causality, denied by Al-Ghazzali's theological assault while vigorously reaffirmed and defended by Ibn-Rushd's equally powerful reply and counter attack.

The whole affair was indeed a rehearsal of things to come on the other side of the divide: like, first, the post-Descartes debates over the problem of natural causality and its relationship to the reality of miracles and to divine causality in the world, issuing in the occasionalism of Malebranche and in David Hume's doctrine of natural causality as no more than habit resulting from the observed constant conjunction of events and the invariable sequence of phenomena. Al-Ghazzali, along with the other Muslim occasionalists, had already arrived at those solutions to the problem and formulated pretty much the same conclusions, particularly the doctrine of "causality as habit" – all in favour of the supremacy of divine causality.

And second, "The Syllabus of Modern Errors", issued by Pope Pius IX in 1864, condemning the set of 80 "most grievous errors, vicious heresy's and depraved innovations" threatening not only Christian orthodoxy as it stood at the time, but also the life of Christendom whole sale.

Among the errors, heresies and innovations condemned, are what the Syllabus then called: scientism, naturalism, materialism, rationalism, secularism, modernism, indifferentism, the cult of religious tolerance

---

[4] *Al-Ghazali's Tahafut Al-Falasifah* (Incoherence of the Philosophers), translated into English by S. A. Kamali, The Pakistan Philosophical Congress, Lahore, first published 1958.
[5] Translated into English by S. Van den Bergh and published under the auspices of the Gibb Memorial Trust, Oxford University Press, 1954.

and so on to the end of the catalogue. And as is well known, the publication of the Syllabus of Errors intensified the general *Kultur Kampf* against the Papacy in Europe in general and in Bismark's Germany in particular.

Western scholars of the modern and contemporary Arab World are aware – but the Western scholarly community in general does not know at all – that less than twenty years after the publication of the Papal Syllabus of Errors, a most dramatic conflict between science and religion was to erupt not in scientifically advancing Europe, but of all places in scientifically innocent and oblivious Beirut, Lebanon or more accurately for those days, in Beirut, Syria under Ottoman rule.

In July 1882, the American physician Edwin Rufus Lewis, graduate of Harvard University Medical School and Professor of Chemistry and Geology at the Syrian Protestant College in Beirut – now famous as the American University of Beirut – delivered the commencement speech before the graduating class of that year and before the entire faculty of the College of those days and in excellent Arabic, under the title of: "Knowledge, Science and Wisdom".

Although the standard missionary, evangelical and religious messages were certainly not absent from that address, Professor Lewis emphasized to the Arab students how only the careful and meticulous application of the scientific method can turn ordinary forms of knowledge into proper scientific truths and transform common experiences into scientifically reliable knowledge and accurate pieces of useful information.

He illustrated his meaning by referring to and praising the work of some great European scientists of the time including Louis Pasteur, Charles Lyelle, the father of modern Geology, Charles Darwin and the new evolutionary biology that he had proposed and instituted. The mention of Charles Darwin was really quite apt at the moment considering that the great scientist had just passed away only 2 months before the delivery of that fateful commencement speech. Still, the shame and scandal were great indeed at the Syrian Protestant College and in the educated circles of Ottoman Beirut, Syria, Mount-Lebanon and British dominated Egypt.[6]

---

[6] The best and fullest account of the Beirut Lewis affair and its reverberations is to be found in S. Jeha's Arabic book, *Darwin and the Crisis of 1882 in the Medical Department of the Syrian Protestant College*, published by the Ras-Beirut Bookshop, Beirut, 1991. English translation by S. Kaya, American University of Beirut Press, Beirut, 2004.

As a result of that favorable mention of Darwin and evolutionary theory, Lewis was dismissed from his teaching post after being accused of heresy, apostasy, atheism, kufr, materialism, corrupting both the minds of the students and the religious faith of the up and coming faculty members and young teachers. He was vigorously and eloquently defended by most of his students, by quite a few of his colleagues on the faculty and by many of the interested local intellectuals of the time – defended on the principle of academic freedom and unhindered scientific research as well as on issues of substance such as openness to new ideas, the local need for scientific progress and the necessity for religious and social enlightenment for Eastern societies.

Actually, the scandal was so grave, the conflict so acute and the crisis so deep that most of the students at the college went on an extended strike (the first of its kind in that part of the world), the best among them were either expelled or left the college on their own initiative, in protest. Many of the most competent and venerable professors at the Syrian Protestant College either resigned or were dismissed on account of their stand vis-à-vis this early conflict of science and religion in Ottoman Beirut. The administration of the College ended up divided against itself and so were the higher Boards of Management and Trustees of the institution. In brief, the college was on the verge of closing itself down and ceasing to exist.

It bears mention here, that some of the students who either left the college in protest or were expelled by way of punishment, proceeded to chart brilliant cultural careers for themselves as thinkers, authors, editors and enlighteners in the Arab World, eventually becoming icons of what is generally known as the Arab Renaissance and the Arab Awakening of that period.

In fact, one of those brilliant students proceeded to become something like the Thomas Huxley of the Arab world – Shibli Shumayyel – in defending Darwin and the case for the science of evolutionary biology, by first providing an Arabic translation of Ludwig Buchner's book on Darwinism (Leipzig 1894), and then producing his own work on the subject. This same line of advanced reasoning, acting and criticizing eventually gave the Arab World – the heartland of Islam – something like a Herbert Spencer in the person and daring progressive works of Salameh Moussa. Moussa later became the main mentor of Naguib Mahfouz, the Arab World's most famous and esteemed novelist and Nobel Laureate for literature.

The ban of "Critique of Religious Thought" (1969)

It also bears a reminder, here, that all this was happening in Beirut long before any one had heard of the American scandal over the teaching of evolutionary biology known as the Scopes trial in the state of Tennessee in 1925 (more popularly known as the Monkey Trial) and certainly still much longer before anyone had paid attention to last year's similar scandal in Dover Pennsylvania (referred to above), not to mention what the Kansas Board of Education was doing, at about the same time, to the teaching of evolutionary theory in that state.[7]

Sometimes, history seems to repeat itself in unexpected ways, at times serious, at other times dramatic and at still other times farcical. So, I beg permission to mention – en passant – that after more than eight decades had passed since the Lewis affair at the Syrian Protestant College, the same institution, now known as the American University of Beirut, had to put up again with another science-religion literary scandal in 1968 and after, known as the al-Azm affair.[8] In that year, I myself was dismissed from my teaching position in the Philosophy Department of the American University of Beirut for messing critically with the question and politics of the conflict of science and religion – both East and West – in my published writings, public lectures and university teaching.

Once more, the *succès de scandale* was great, the controversies loud and noisy, the divisions deep, the polemics massive (over 1,500 pages of published materials), the trial extended, the threats menacing and the accusations all too familiar: heresy, apostasy, materialism, atheism, kufr corrupting the youth and so on. One of the criminalized essays carried the following title: "Scientific Culture and the Poverty of Religious Thought". The book collecting all these essays was published at the end of 1969 under the title: *Critique of Religious Thought,* banned everywhere in the Arab world (except Lebanon), available everywhere around the Arab World and never out of print since then.[9]

Let me add that long before the current discourses about the clash of civilizations, the dialogue of cultures, religions and faiths etc. went into wide circulation nationally and internationally, Beirut was already

---

[7] See note 2.
[8] For a full account of the al-Azm affair, see, S. Wild, "Gott und Mensch im Libanon: Die Affäre Sadiq al-'Azm", *Der Islam*, Band 48, Heft 2, 1972, 206-253.
[9] Sadiq Jalal al-Azm, *Critique of Religious Thought*, Tali'a Publications, Beirut, first printing 1969. Translations to English and French of the book are currently underway in the US and France respectively.

preoccupied in the middle of the Sixties by what was then known as the Muslim- Christian dialogue.[10] I myself attacked the exercise for its futility and for the hypocrisy of the two sides engaged in it. In any case, it proved to be a prelude to and a preparation for the long Lebanese civil war soon to explode rather than the start of a new era of improved mutual Christian-Muslim understanding in Lebanon. My primary point in criticizing the dialogue was that neither side really wanted to give secular autonomous reason a chance to act as the regulative principle for and of the whole activity and as a main reference point for sorting out areas of genuine agreement, areas of total but honest disagreement, areas of both honestly and dishonestly dissimulated agreements and disagreements, areas of overlap and possible agreement and conciliation to be worked out through the dialogue. Instead, each side kept reciting its own faith-based claims in the form of what it thought were reasonable propositions. Each side came to the dialogue with an absolute rejection of the possibility, extremely remote as it may be, that it might be partially wrong, at least about some of the details of the other side's religious convictions and positions.

Now, a certain problem imposes itself on our attention: we all know that during at least the last two centuries very little science of any kind was conducted in the Islamic World and that hardly any sort of scientific knowledge was produced in Muslim countries or by Muslim societies of any sort. If so, then why should big and small conflicts over the issue of the opposition between modern science and ancient religion erupt in cultures and places like Beirut, Cairo and Istanbul where until today there is hardly any significant science or serious scientific activity of consequence going on, in the first place?

In the following, I shall present some considerations that, I think, will shed some light on this problem and help in partially answering the question.

Although, the scientific revolution and its accompaniments is of modern European origin and provenance – conventionally traced back and attributed to such episodes in modern European history as the Renaissance, the 17th century mathematization of nature and the Enlightenment – the overall knowledge-model that grew out of that revolution came very quickly to acquire a universal human significance and sweep that transcends its humble, localized European origins and that made of it everywhere the compelling and pervasive normative

---

[10] *Christianity and Islam in Lebanon*, Lebanese Nadwa Publications, Beirut, 1965 (in Arabic).

paradigm on all matters pertaining to the acquisition, production, distribution, use and application of knowledge in the realms of the natural, the social and the human in general. This paradigm comprises: (a) science as a method of systematic inquiry, discovery, invention and verification, (b) science as an accumulated and accumulating body of reliable knowledge about the natural, social and human spheres and (c) science as applied technology and transformative technique.

Actually, I would like to go as far as claiming that no previous knowledge-model in the history of humanity – be it religious, revealed, secular, or otherwise – has been able to achieve the kind of paradigmatic universality, hegemony, comprehensiveness, legitimacy, strength and efficacy that this modern scientific knowledge-model succeeded in attaining. This is why I think that all talk today about the Islamization, Africanization, Hinduisation etc. of knowledge, simply constitutes an additional affirmation of the global primacy attained by the original knowledge – paradigm that emerged and crystallized out of the primary scientific revolution in Europe.

In other words, if Goethe could speak in his own time of an emerging universal world literature (his *Welt Literature*) transcending national limits, cultural boundaries and provincial traditions, we should be able to speak, just as legitimately and convincingly in our own time of a reigning world scientific knowledge-paradigm that transcends even more thoroughly and effectively national limits, cultural boundaries, provincial traditions and local forms of knowledge, both practical and theoretical.

This leads me to conclude that the conflicts, controversies and fights between science and religion that erupted and continue to erupt in scientifically insignificant places like Beirut, Cairo and Istanbul go back to the clash of this by now inescapable universal knowledge-paradigm with the religion-based forms of knowledge and ways of appropriating, interpreting and acting on the world. The resulting crisis is aggravated by the fact that as various Muslim societies, for example, reach out for development, seek economic progress and acquire additional scientific–technical skills through the appropriation, reproduction and use of this dominant knowledge-paradigm then inevitably such conflicts will not only surface but will also explode into major confrontations, controversies and polemics over issues of the compatibility of science and religion, reason and revelation and so on. In this process, the new type of knowledge will tend to marginalise the earlier forms of appropriating, interpreting and acting on the world such as myth, magic, religion, legend, affective encounter, scholastic reason and the rest.

In fact, already the natural, social, human and legal sciences have come to dominate school and university curricula in almost all Muslim states and Arab countries wresting primacy of place from the traditional religious sciences and forms of learning. This is one major loss to traditional Islam that today's fundamentalists are violently reacting against and trying to, at least partially, retrieve.

Impeding the creativity of novelists, poets, etc.

Another interesting feature of these societies where serious science is almost completely absent is the fact that the incongruities, paradoxes, absurdities and tensions attendant on the science-religion conflict are systematically explored and exposed not so much on the terrain of science itself but rather in such forms as: general cultural critiques, enlightenment kind of projects, attempts at religio-theological reform and creative literary productions, with special emphasis on the novel and without excluding even poetry.

Let me say something, first, about religious-theological reform. In the Arab world, the encounter with and the impact of this new knowledge-paradigm, with all its manifest implications and superior applications, was one decisive factor in the making of the great movement of liberal reform and latitudinarian religious interpretation that Arab life and thought witnessed towards the last quarter of the 19th Century. This movement has been variously called by ourselves as well as by Western scholars: an awakening, a renaissance, a religious reformation, the liberal experiment, Muslim modernism and the liberal age of modern Arab thought. And in fact, the movement did compress in itself all at once a quasi theologico-legal reformation, a literary-intellectual renaissance, a rational-scientific enlightenment of sorts and a political and ideological aggiornamento as well.

This encounter and impact was decisive in driving Arab and Muslim intellectuals, observers, reformers, students, travelers etc. throughout the second half of the 19th century to follow with great interest Europe's critiques of religion, such as carried out by the Spinoza's, Voltaires, Marxes, Nietzsches, Freuds, Darwins, Huxleys etc.. , setting out to learn, among other things, lessons about pressing issues like the conflict of science and religion in the West, the place of religious belief in secularizing social orders, the function and fate of religious scriptures in a modern scientific and technological age and so on.

For example, Jamaluddin Al-Afghani, the towering personality of that moment, carried on a famous correspondence with Europe's then all purpose scholar and most noted public intellectual Ernest Renan on such matters as the conflict of science and religion, the place of religious belief in a secular social order and the role of religion in general and of Islam in particular in impeding both scientific and social progress.[11]

In 1885, when Afghani visited London, he stayed with the English Orientalist, traveller and author Wilfrid Blunt, the dominant topics of their consultations and discussions were naturally politics, science and religion. The same Wilfrid Blunt maintained a very close personal and intellectual association with the other towering personality of the Arab Renaissance period, Mohamed Abdu-the great latitudinarian theologian and re-interpreter of Islam – especially during Blunt's long stays in Cairo. Interestingly enough, Blunt himself had lost his Roman Catholic faith after studying Darwin's Origin of Species and left the following remark about his prominent Muslim friend: "I fear he has as little faith in Islam as I have in the Catholic Church." Abdu and Blunt made a pilgrimage together to Brighton, England to converse with and learn from none other than the most famous Darwinian of the day, Herbert Spencer.[12]

I move now to the realm of the literary since, as I hinted earlier, the novel constitutes one major medium where the science-religion conflict got dealt with excellently and explosively. For example, the literary works of Egypt's Nobel Laureate Naguib Mahfouz abound with treatments of the topic in a whole variety of settings, idioms, contexts and dramatizations. His famous novel Gabalawi's Children – also translated more literally as The Children of Our Alley – is devoted solely to that subject. The story line starts with characters like Adham (i.e., Adam) and Idriss (i.e., Iblees or Diabolos) and reaches its climax in a sort of Nietzschean revelation that the ancient and long concealed Gabalawi (i.e., God) had either died at the hands of modern science or was exposed as an inexistent, but still powerful and persistent, myth by a new character called 'Arafeh, i.e., the One Who Knows or The Knower' (at the same time the name of the mountain near Mecca where

---

[11] N.R. Keddie (ed.), *An Islamic Response to Imperialism: Political and Religious Writings of Sayyed Jamal al-Din-'al Afghani*; University of California Press, 1983. Also, E. Kedourie, *Afghani and Abdu: An Essay on Religious Unbelief and Political Activism in Islam*, Frank Cass & Co, London, 1966.

[12] See, A. Hourani's essay, "Wilfrid Scawen Blunt and the Revival of the East" in his book, *Europe and the Middle East*, The Macmillan Press, 1980, pp. 87-103.

Muslim pilgrims stand and perform prayers during the Hajj season. In literature names are never innocent).

To drive his point home, Mahfouz constructed the novel into 115 chapters, exactly the number of chapters (or suras) out of which the *Qur'ân* is made including the opening Lord's Prayer, known as the Fatiha. The novel has been denounced and banned by Al-Azhar since its first incomplete publication in Cairo in 1957, but as is usual in the Arab World it is readily available everywhere. And as is well known, Mahfouz mercifully survived an assassination attempt in Cairo in 1994, by an operative of one of the fundamentalist Islamic organizations active in Egypt at the time. He just passed away while the novel got passed by Al-Azhar and we have now an Egyptian printing of it.

Another relevant novelistic treatment of the subject is to be found in the early pages of Salman Rushdie's Midnight's Children, devoted to the tragi-comic incongruities, paradoxes and absurdities of Adam Aziz, a Kashmiri modern trained physician who had read Lenin's What is to be done? at the University of Heidelberg, trying to practice his modern art and newly acquired scientific knowledge from behind a perforated sheet on a veiled feudal female in the backwoods of Kashmir.

Already, about a half century ago one of Egypt's most eminent men of letters had published a similar allegory about the tragedy of Ismaïl Efendi, a modern trained Egyptian Doctor who returns from London to practice his art on, among others, an illiterate female relative in his extremely materially depressed and highly superstitious village.[13] Just as Adam Aziz had somehow to carry on with the treatment in spite of the perforated sheet Islamically standing between him and his patient, similarly Dr. Ismaïl had to somehow carry on with his treatment in spite of the magical lantern Islamically standing between him and his sick cousin. Like Galileo in Bertolt Brecht's famous play, both Dr. Ismaïl and Dr. Aziz shun the heroic path of Giordano Bruno, make the compromises necessary for the continuation of their work – a work that historically transcends their individual destinies – and for the eventual triumph of what they stand for. Both doctors end up marrying their illiterate and superstitious patients.

Obviously, then, the authors and books referred to above generate reactions because they honestly and boldly either explore, expose, criticize or parody the conflicts, incongruities, contradictions, paradoxes, absurdities and tensions attendant on this paradigm clash and shift.

---

[13] Y. Haqi, *Um Hashim's Lantern*, Cairo, 1944. English translation: *The Lamp of Um Hashim and other Stories*, American University in Cairo Press, Cairo, 2004.

In this genre also, the most celebrated instance is of course Salman Rushdie's most famous novel The Satanic Verses and the unprecedented global literary scandal, affair and crisis it generated. During his ordeal, Rushdie thought for a moment that he could somehow escape the consequences of the death sentence issued against him by Imam Khomeini – known as the *Fatwa* – by declaring to the world that he has come around to embrace Islam (1990). But when this tricky embracing of Islam did not work, Rushdie recanted his recantation in a lecture at Colombia University in New York (1991), and went back to his original defiant position against the forces of religious fundamentalism, fanaticism, censorship and oppression. I mention all this because it all profitably brought back to me the Galileo affair and trial.[14]

More specifically, it seemed to me that Rushdie's first recantation was as insincere, coerced and utilitarian as Galileo's. As we all know by now, the persecuted father of modern physics recanted his recantation, not only when he supposedly whispered "it moves", but ultimately when he gave the world his most mature work, Dialogues on the New Sciences composed behind the backs of the Church censors, watching his every move, and smuggled it out of Italy to Holland for publication under the nose of the Inquisition. Similarly, Rushdie recanted his recantation, not only when he gave his lecture at Columbia University, but also when he overcame the terror of the "*Fatwa*" threatening to undo him by not ceasing to write satirically, critically and creatively, particularly about the sacred.

In fact, this analogy acquires greater cogency on the basis of the authoritative study of the Galileo case by Pietro Redondi, Galileo Heretico.[15] Redondi argues that the Church condemned Galileo not so much for his Copernicanism, i.e., his cosmology, as for the explosive implications of his new physics, mainly his atomism, for the doctrine of transubstantiation. This came at a perilous time for the Church when the doctrine in question was under attack by rising Protestantism and its rival doctrine of consubstantiation. We all know something by now about the subversive and explosive implications of Rushdie's art for the comparably sacred Islamic scholastic doctrines and narratives, and at a particularly perilous time for an eroding Islam before the forces of modernity.

---

[14] See, S. Rushdie's "Why I have Embraced Islam", *Imaginary Homelands*, Granta Books, 1991, and his "One Thousand Days in a Balloon", *The Rushdie Letters*, ed. by S. Macdonogh, University of Nebraska Press, 1993.

[15] P. Redondi, *Galileo Heretico*, translated from Italian by R. Rosenthal, Princeton University Press, 1989.

Of interest also is the fact that not unlike Rushdie, Galileo wrote some of his more controversial works in the epico-satiric style of fiery literary polemics, taking on none other than the Collegio Romano itself. In fact, this is pretty much the style of Rushdie's Literary productions and particularly The Satanic Verses. Let me add that it was Galileo who first defined carnival as the time and place where it is permissible to speak freely about everything. And the Satanic Verses is nothing if it is not carnivalesque to the core and if it is not free speech about everything.

It is worth mentioning here as well that it was only in November 1992, that the Catholic Church formally admitted having done anything wrong to Galileo. It took the commission appointed by Pope John Paul II to review the condemnation of the great scientist in 1633, 13 years to reach the conclusion that "we today know that Galileo was right in adopting the Copernican astronomical theory"[16]. I wonder if Islam will have to wait another 3 to 5 hundred years before making a similar admission about Rushdie and his novel.

Can Islam reconcile itself with the new and dominant scientific knowledge-paradigm?

Finally, let me ask the question: can Islam ever reconcile itself with this new and reigning scientific knowledge-paradigm and/or model? I do not think there is a simple either Yes or No answer to this question. The answer has to be a historically based dialectical yes and no at one and the same time.

I should immediately point out that this question has been, in a whole variety of formulations, idioms and ways, on the agenda of Arab and Muslim thought and history for the last 200 years. Certainly, we Arabs have been interrogating ourselves, in many a way and form, about its implications and applications for ourselves and for our relationship to the rest of the world for no less than 150 years.

Now, any one taking his cues at present from the classical movement of liberal reform and latitudinarian religious interpretation in Arab life and thought and regards himself as its descendant and heir will give a confident affirmative Yes, for an answer to our question. At the same time anyone taking his cues from the classical movement of Islamic counter-reform as represented in the programs of the Muslim Brothers Organization and the condemnatory fundamentalist ideology of the

---

[16] As expressed in an interview by Cardinal P. Poupard, the head of the investigating Papal Commission, *The New York Times*, October 31, 1992.

Jahiliya[17] of the 20th Century and beyond, will certainly answer the same question with an emphatic and unequivocal No.

In other words, the Yes faction descends from the likes of Jamaluddine Al-Afaghani and Mohamed Abdu of the Arab awakening and renaissance period; while the No faction of today descends from the likes of Egypt's founder of the Muslim Brothers Organization in 1928, Hasan Al-Banna, India's Abu-al A'la al-Mawdudi, the master theoretician of reactive Fundamentalist Islam in the 20th Century and from Sayyed Qutub, the author of the founding text and primary manifesto of *Jihad*ist Islam in the second half of the 20th Century.[18]

The following is one set of examples of how the No faction argues and thinks about the question of science and religion, drawn from the writings of Shukri Mustafa, leader of the Fundamentalist Islamist Organization in Egypt known as the Excommunication and Emigration Group:

(1) "I say, he who thinks that the burdens of building modern civilization are not in conflict with the commandments of worshipping God, and he who thinks it is possible for the Western scientists and builders of civilization to be also obedient servants of God at one and the same time, simply testifies to his own shamelessness and insolence, for they [the Western scientists] are the ones who have forsaken the other world in favor of this one."

(2) "Was it really possible for the Prophet Muhammad and his companions – the hermits of the night and knights of the day, in God's service – to be also physicists, mathematicians, pioneers of space exploration and makers of modern civilization?"

(3) "For thirteen years in Mecca, Allah's Prophet taught the Muslims Islam and nothing but Islam, neither astronomy, nor mathematics, nor physics, nor philosophy; where are those impostors who claim that Islam cannot be established unless it becomes a pupil of the European sciences?"

(4) "Concerning the question of science (knowledge), it remains for me to say that the whole of humanity that went astray and that God destroyed, prided itself above God through nothing but the fruits of a science, cut off from the worship of God alone and no one else."[19]

---

[17] *Jahiliya* is the age of ignorance, idolatry and Godlessness that preceded the rise of Islam in Arabia.

[18] See, A.S. Mussalli, *Moderate and Radical Islamic Fundamentalism*, University Press of Florida, 1999.

[19] My own translation from the Arabic original. See my essay: "Islamic Fundamentalism Reconsidered", *South Asia Bulletin: Comparative Studies of South Asia, Africa and the Middle East*, vol. 13, Nos. 1 & 2, 1993 and vol. 14, No. 1, 1994.

Science And Religion

The late Abdul-Aziz Bin Baz, the Grand Mufti and master Faqih of the Saudi Arabian Kingdom and the chief of its clerical power structure for long years, handed the No faction a left-handed compliment by publishing a book in 1982 bearing the following long and self-explanatory title: The Traditional and Perceptual Proofs for the Possibility of Ascending to the Planets, for the Motion of the Sun and Moon and for the Fixity of the Earth.

Bin Baz, took it upon himself to expound and defend in this book a cosmology based purely on the *Qur'ân*, the Sunna and the ancient Muslim authorities. Naturally, the results were:
(a) A reaffirmation of the flatness of the earth.
(b) A reassertion of Geocentrism.
(c) A condemnation to apostasy and kufr of all Muslims who believe that the earth is round and revolves around the sun.
(d) A reminder to all concerned that the punishment for apostasy and kufr in Islam is death.

The more moderate and realistic Islamist trends take a more sophisticated approach in negotiating the science-religion problem and mediating the conflict inherent in it.
First, Scientific knowledge is underrated and disparaged by turning its very distinguishing characteristics against it. In other words, the fact that scientific knowledge is always incomplete, cumulative, approximative, contingent, corrigible, falsifiable, revisable and so on, renders it "not real knowledge" in their eyes. Knowledge, for them is always of the Truth, while the known truths are not Real Knowledge.

Second, science is stripped of all significant theoretico-epistemological value and cognitive content by reducing it to not much more than sets of successful guesses, useful calculations, practical techniques and effective operations for the manipulation of material objects and the satisfaction of human needs. As far as science is concerned, these Islamists come out as enthusiastic partisans of primitive operationalism and crude technicism. The more sophisticated theoreticians among them tend to add a dash of fashionable conventionalism and pragmatic instrumentalism.

All in all, I can safely say that in practice they clumsily and unknowingly heed the substance of the advice Cardinal Bellarmino once gave to Galileo in order to avoid head-on-collision with the fundamentals of the then reigning Roman Catholic Orthodoxy and its guardians. According to that cunning piece of advice Galileo had to stop affirming that his scientific inquiries were producing knowledge about the nature of the world (true propositions about floating bodies, sun spots, vacua, the motion of the earth, the moons of Jupiter and the mutability of celestial matter), in favor of only claiming that his science proposes no more than, (a) useful "hypotheses" that allow us to handle physical phenomena more effectively and efficiently, and (b) practical mathematical calculations, formulae and tricks for the improved manipulation of objects, their motions and relations. Of course, "hypotheses" are to be taken, here, in the older pejorative sense repudiated by Isaac Newton, qua scientist, in his famous denial: "Hypotheses non-fingo".

In other words, Galileo was advised to leave the truth about the affairs of this world also – and not just the other one – to established religion by confining himself, as scientist, to the production of interesting speculations, useful hypotheses and practical calculations, but no more. The devaluation of the theoretico-cognitive significance of science and modern scientific knowledge in general is given by Ayatollah Mutahhari in the following words:

"Another shortcoming of the scientific world view as a basis for an ideology is that science is unstable and unenduring from a theoretical standpoint, that is, from the standpoint of presenting reality as it is or of attracting faith to the nature of the reality of being. From the viewpoint of science, the face of the world changes from day to day because science is based on hypothesis and experiment, not on rational and self-evident first principles. Hypothesis and experiment have a provisional value; so the scientific worldview is shaky and inconsistent and cannot serve as a foundation for faith. Faith demands a firmer, an unshakable foundation, a foundation characterized by eternity... The importance of the scientific worldview lies in its practical, technical value, not in its theoretical value. What can serve as the support for an ideology is a theoretical value, not a practical one... The practical and technical value of science lies in science's empowering man in his work and being fruitful, whether or not it represents reality. Today's industry and technology display the practical and technical value of science." Then the Ayatollah concludes that:

"One of the remarkable things about science in today's world is that, to the extent that its practical and technical value increases, its theoretical value diminishes".[20]

---

[20] Ayatollah Murtaza Mutahhari, *Fundamentals of Islamic Thought: God, Man and the Universe*, translated from Persian by R. Campbell, Mizan Press, California, 1985.

Now, what do I make out of this impasse between the Yes faction and the No faction within the house of Islam? I make conceptual sense out of this seeming deadlock by arguing that Islam as a coherent static ideal of eternal and permanently valid principles cannot reconcile itself with the new and dominant scientific knowledge-paradigm, like any other major religion viewed under the aspect of eternity. But Islam as a living, dynamic evolving faith responding to widely differing environments, rapidly shifting historical circumstances and continuously developing knowledge-models and paradigms will always find practical, temporary and ad hoc forms of reconciliation and accommodation with the reigning scientific reason of the day – exactly as it had done before throughout its long history as a survival strategy.

Conclusion

In scientifically vibrant and productive societies, science and religion are kept separate. From the beginning this was a pragmatic measure that on the whole succeeded in maintaining the peace, but not wholly, fully and all the time. Scientifically backward and deeply religious societies cannot aspire as yet to a successful and effective implementation of a similar measure. For them, the fight continues.

Response by Mark Eyskens

Professor Sadik al-Azm has given us a masterful sketch of the way in which the conflict between religion and science is unique to the three monotheistic religions: Judaism, Christianity and Islam.

Monotheism arose at the beginning of the second millennium before Christ in the midst of a small desert tribe of nomads known as the Hebrews, who led the trading caravans between the major cities of ancient Mesopotamia, such as Akkad, Sumer and Ur, and the Persian Gulf. Monotheism developed as a reaction to the widespread and very complex polytheism, in which the numerous gods were considered to embody the forces of nature which human beings found themselves confronted with. Freud and contemporary biblical scholars reject the view that the Egyptian pharaoh Akhenaton – who initiated a sort of monotheistic cult of the sun – was the precursor of the Jewish monotheism propagated by Moses from Egypt. The monotheistic conception of God as a great Being who gives a universal, general revelation of reality is a revolutionary idea. To this day, believers affirm that their faith comes from a divine revelation, while non-believers claim that monotheism was an ingenious human idea. The ingeniousness lies in the introduction into human thought of a concept of oneness that offers unity and a worldview that is constructed vertically from an all-powerful God who is 'Creator of heaven and earth'. Yahweh is, according to the burning bush definition in the Old Testament, 'he who is', a nearly abstract definition that points to the ineffability of the mystery of being. This abstract vision of God is not, of course, one that will guarantee popularity, and in the Old Testament it became humanised by giving the non-figurative concept of the divine the profile of a human father, a ruler over heavenly hosts, a strict judge of good and evil, a lawmaker who hands his commandments down to humanity and makes them obligatory through an ethic of reward and punishment.

The monotheistic conception of God developed, of course, in the pre-scientific period of human thought. The creation story and the entry of Yahweh into the history of the Jewish people were self-evident to the people of Israel and considered a basic datum of experience. That the word of God was revealed through prophets and recorded in their holy books was taken for granted, as was the belief that the Old (and later the New) Testament contained indisputable truth. This view carried through seamlessly into the Christianity of the Church Fathers, and even into the reasoning of great theologians and philosophers such as Augustine and St Thomas. According to them, there is but one indivisible truth, and human reason must necessarily reach the same conclusions as what is written in Holy Scripture. Muhammad, in the revelation he received directly from the archangel Gabriel, proclaimed the same belief that at that time was deemed self-evident.

The conflict between science and faith arose with the awakening of scientific thought, reinforced by empirical investigation, especially when it became apparent that certain biblical notions such as that the earth was at the centre of the universe did not agree with scientific perception. The consequences with Galileo, Giordano Bruno and much later Darwin are well known.

The rise of science demystified the image of the world and unmasked the mythical nature of religion – more particularly of monotheism with its creation story and divine interventionism. This immediately led to a great scandal that is still raging, with actions and reactions from on the one hand exclusively materialistic scientists such as the biologist Richard Dawkins and, on the other hand, fundamentalist creationists.

For many Western thinkers, the battle between science and religion, between knowledge and belief, has to a large extent been won. Within Islam, however, the priority of the holy book, the *Qur'ân*, continues, and the divine truth held to be revealed therein takes precedence over all other forms of human knowledge.

Prof. al-Azm rightly cites the famous 'Syllabus of Errors' of Pope Pius IX, published in 1864, in which the pontiff condemns a whole series of propositions deemed heretical, including the separation of church and State, and democracy. For authority comes from almighty God and therefore cannot arise within society by means of democratic elections. The State and the community must be governed in accordance with the principles revealed by God. In this view, the separation of State and religion amounts to a negation of God's existence, and is thus intrinsically atheistic. This Catholic dogmatism of scarcely 150 years ago is today shared to a considerable extent by Islamic religious leaders and is applied in most Muslim countries. It could thus be argued that the conflictual relationship between religion and science in the Islam is a matter of a chronological delay. Within the Christian churches – cf. the writings of the Church Fathers and theologians such as St Thomas – it was once held that science could at best be the handmaid of theology. It played an ancillary role. But under the influence of the information and communication revolution currently under way, in Muslim countries as elsewhere, the tension between faith and science will gradually disappear.

In Western thought, creationism and 'intelligent design' are reactionary regurgitations that are no more than a rearguard action. Creationism is a desperate return to a mythological explanation of reality. 'Intelligent design' appears to be a more reasonable approach. It is evident that nature operates in a most ingenious manner, so that the idea of a plan and purpose arises spontaneously. Modern science also demonstrates that chance and necessity are very closely related to each other. It appears as well that nature uses the method of trial and error, and that blunders of various sorts also appear in nature. Call it 'stupid design' if you will. Hence we have the law of entropy, which is a general law of nature: the law of decline, of decomposition, of disorder, chaos and ultimately death. Everything in nature breaks down. Not only human, animal and plant life but even mother earth itself, for in 4 billion years it will be burned up by our exploding sun, and billions of years later our Milky Way will be pulverised like other galaxies before it. The imperfection of creation is experienced above all in human existence. Human beings are plagued by countless diseases and die for the most part in a very painful manner. All this runs counter to the notion of an intelligent design and confronts human beings with the agonizing enigma of evil, pain and suffering in their very existence.

Modern cosmology and quantum physics have reached the conclusion that reality has neither a beginning nor an end. Being is being. Period. The expression 'there is nothing' is nonsensical, for this statement situates 'nothing' in 'being'. Being is thus absolute in the literal sense of the word; it is all-encompassing. Time and space are situated within being, and not the other way around. A first cause is impossible, for this presumes a sequence from A to B, which can only happen within timespace, since one of the characteristics of being is that it cannot be situated outside of being.

Monotheistic believers are upset by the painful but insoluble paradox that appears when the concept of the divine insists on an almighty, creator God who is at the same time infinitely loving, in a world where humanity is marked by abysmal evil, inexpressible suffering and catastrophic disasters. The Catholic Church has never been able to formulate an adequate response to this problem. Islam, like Christianity, explains evil and suffering as a punishment from Allah, which should be considered beneficial as a radical way of stamping out behaviour that is deemed sinful.

In contemporary Western thought, there is for the most part a definitive ceasefire, if not a sort of 'peace of God' between theology and science, thanks to the complete separation (independence) that has arisen between scientific knowledge and religious belief. The Church states that science is concerned with the 'how questions' and religion with the 'why questions'. This distinction seems to me somewhat simplistic. It is indisputable that in science as well, why questions arise. I would think it more accurate to say that science is concerned with explaining reality and with changing that reality via successive technological revolutions that provide for an increasing well-being. Religion, on the other hand, does not concern itself with explaining reality – that task is the prerogative of science – but with improving reality, that is to say, with humanising this scientifically driven progress.

Propositions

For the believing Jew, Christian and Muslim, a new theological vision is necessary, in my view, in the face of the confrontation with but also as a result of the integration of essential scientific insights into religion. This new vision I would venture to express as follows.

1. The monotheistic conception of God must be demystified. According to modern science, there is no beginning and no end, for time lies within being and not outside of it. There is thus neither a first cause nor a first creation. Within being, there are certainly creations and changes. This view represents a break with the notion of an almighty God who, like some transcendent demiurge, brings being into the world and regulates it from a distance.

2. The decausalisation of the concept of God unravels the paradox of suffering and evil with which humans are confronted as long as God is seen as both all-powerful and infinitely loving. This gives the declaration in the gospel of John that 'God is love' its revolutionary and fundamental meaning. The loving God struggles with people of good will against evil and pain, suffering and injustice, sickness and death. The God of love and the love of God thus recreate reality. God makes all things new. This God is not far away but very near. I would not call him transcendent but rather transmanent, a combination of transcendence and immanence. The recreation of reality through divine love is not a physical but a metaphysical process.

3. Unselfish love (love your neighbour, even your enemy), goodness, justice, the quest for truth and beauty are not found in nature. The animal world is terribly violent as a result of the 'struggle for life' and the 'survival of the fittest'. Unselfish love, goodness, justice and beauty thus appear to be unnatural virtues – call them supernatural or divine – as Plato had already asserted. These divine virtues 'are' but they do not 'exist' unless they are incarnated in good people. This is the source of the theological concept of the incarnation of the divine, of the God who becomes man, as Christians believe, in the person of Jesus. The incarnation can take other forms and symbolic formulations in other religions as well. For Christians, the message of Jesus – for Muslim believers the message expressed by Mohammed and for Jews that of the prophets – is a radical one, one that creates meaning.

4. The message of love proclaimed by Christ is the diametrical opposite of the law of a selfish 'struggle for life', a necessity for both humans and animals during the history of their evolution. Christ came to proclaim that this sort of egoism brings death and destruction to humanity. Two thousand years later, now that human beings have weapons of mass destruction, this message is more relevant than ever. Jesus thus

saves humans from their fatal egoism (represented in the Bible by the questionable concept of original sin).

5. The Christian message receives its full, revolutionary meaning when one comes to the realisation that theological concepts such as salvation, resurrection, heaven, eternal life, blessedness are references to what I would like to call transcendent evolutionism. Human existence is marked by three mega-events: a transcendent triad. First, the coming to life of inorganic matter – vitalisation – by the emergence of the first primitive cell around three and a half billion years ago. This is the beginning of biological evolution on earth. Next, around eight million years ago, another colossal transformation took place, also through a gradual process, namely the hominisation of animals. Both the vitalisation of matter and the hominisation of animal life have now been thoroughly unravelled and explained by science. The message of salvation, certainly within the monotheistic religions and more specifically in Christianity, formulates a third and final stage in this evolution. This stage I would call the divinisation or deification of the good human being, who has experienced and integrated the supernatural virtues of love, goodness, justice and the quest for truth and beauty into his or her life. This divinisation is similar to what Teilhard de Chardin called the 'Omega point' as the end point of evolution.

6. The theological circle is thus closed. There is the incarnation of God and the deification of humans. The God of love is incarnate in good people and struggles along with them – through falling and arising again – against evil and pain, against injustice, disease and death. Love recreates reality into a meta-reality in which good people are taken up into a sort of meta-existence, characterised by a quality of being that brings them closer to God. The divinisation or blessedness in a meta-life that is also a meta-death cannot be expressed in words. Thus it is evident that Holy Scripture can never be taken literally.

God is thus no longer the first cause, but rather the final goal of human existence. The decausalisation of the concept of God leads to a finalising of the concept of God. God is no longer 'the great creator' but rather 'the great attractor'. He is not a physical creator, but a recreator of reality through divine love.

7. The beautiful, highly poetic creation story of Genesis must therefore be read in an entirely different way. This text is not about the first beginnings, but calls forth a vision of the future of humanity. The

human being will be created in God's image and likeness. The good person receives a divine destiny with which he can break through the law of entropy – including death. This is what gives human existence its fundamental meaning in a message of hope that transcends existential contingencies.

Response by Roger Dillemans

Like all of us, I suppose, I was impressed by the lecturer's historical review, but particularly by his revealing insight into the current problem of the relationship between science and religion, both here in Europe and in the Islamic countries. And by his innovative and creative point of view and courageous attitude.

In traditional Islam, the course of human development is highly determined and there can be no opposition between science and religion. However, some contemporary English-speaking philosophical scientists of Islamic origin, like most of the speakers at this Forum, plead in favour of true creativity, the impact of science, and freedom of research.

The relationship between science and religion, and particularly their combination, has indeed always been a difficult issue in the monotheistic traditions. As far as Europe is concerned, the universities that call themselves Catholic are of course directly concerned.

Some fifteen years ago I participated in a meeting in Amman of a delegation of European university rectors and of rectors/presidents of universities in Islamic countries. The atmosphere was warm and friendly, and we all behaved as true colleagues, with the necessary openness for discussion. We ended up, though, with the strange and strong feeling that we represented rather different types of institutions. Whereas religion was not a real issue for the European delegates, it was regularly mentioned by our Islamic counterparts in relation to both education and scientific research. Clearly, their views on both of these tasks were inspired by religion.

Some rectors/presidents asserted that they were getting away from former closed traditions and moving towards the internationally recognized mandate and status of free research supporting education. And, indeed, in several universities freedom of research was guaranteed in most fields of science. We concluded by committing ourselves, reciprocally, to setting up opportunities for exchanges of academic staff, researchers and promising students in the future. I am not sure that very much came out of it.

As to the question of what a university really should be, we in this part of the world (Europe) draw our inspiration from the famous 'Magna Charta of European Universities' signed in Bologna in 1988, which is endorsed by most European universities as well as by numerous universities outside Europe: the university is an autonomous institution that produces and transfers knowledge through a combination of free research and teaching.

How does the Bologna mission statement apply to the universities that call themselves Catholic? Here, of course, a serious question arises: how can Catholic universities reconcile that identity with freedom of research – taking for granted that there is no true research without freedom of research, conducted in a free state of mind without any other aim than to seek the truth, the final reality of things and of humankind?

At about the same period as the Amman meeting I was, as rector of the Catholic University of Louvain (Leuven), invited - not urged - to come to a broad international meeting in Rome, in order to collaborate on drafting a sort of statutory text on the identity of Catholic universities.

My first question, very spontaneously, at this meeting was to ask for a preliminary clarification: what is a university? Evidently, I invoked the Bologna statement.

The assembly was split into two rather different groups. Of course there are a number of 'Catholic universities' in the world. Some are huge institutions, larger than the Catholic University of Louvain and certainly more 'catholic', but have a different view of what a university should be. In what came out as an 'apostolic constitution', under the title "Ex corde ecclesiae" (1990) - for the first time as far as I can remember - freedom of research was officially recognized as essential to the identity of universities. We were proud of this outcome and happy to report back home. However, we were less happy when we eventually discovered in the final version of the document that by some vague sort of exception, a special status was reserved for one particular science: theology. It was said that the few 'Catholic universities' worthy of that name (that were left – in Europe and the U.S.) would never agree to give up that crucial element of freedom of research, and that the Vatican was used to living in a situation of continued tension with them, especially on ethical issues such as those which arise in the bio-medical fields. But the Pope himself and his entourage seemed to be more concerned with the position taken by certain renowned theologians, especially in Germany and the Low Countries.

In reality, all of us who engage in research at these Catholic universities claim full freedom of research but, at the same time, many remain faithful to the project of a Catholic university that is based on Christian inspiration. That inspiration implies that we are pursuing the work of 'creation' in an attempt to make our world and society a better and more humane place to live. As we have now entered the 'knowledge society', research is one of the main tasks of humanity, so that engaging in research is itself of a high ethical value. And this has nothing to do with 'creationism' or 'intelligent design'. We cannot but accept the scientific conclusions of the Newtons, the Darwins, the Einsteins and Heisenbergs of modern science. But Darwin does not forbid us to 'believe' that God was at the beginning of it all. What matters is that we do not represent that God by means of simplified human images or with a facile anthropomorphism.

Western societies today agree that science and religion are two different views of humanity (as is the case with art and moral attitudes). Both are worthwhile, complementary and can be combined in the same person. Science seeks the answer to the question of what reality is. Religion can provide inspiration for the question of why the world is as it is.[21] Since the Enlightenment in Western Europe, believers have come to accept the results of scientific research. Scientists, in turn, concede today that they will probably never find the final answers to the essential questions of why and where to.

Science has never discovered anything that is bad or wrong in itself. Of course, Christian ethics can inspire and guide us 1) in the methodology we adopt, 2) in the ultimate use we make of our discoveries and even 3) in the choices we make as to which fields are worth focusing our research efforts upon.

Christianity is probably the religion that, compared to other religions, after many dark ages, shows itself most willing to respect the role of science and to accept its results, even if in some cases this occurs only after a long delay. In the case of Catholicism, the Vatican's concern has more to do with moral principles (some of which are outdated) and their applications. And indeed, there are certain limits of the type I have mentioned here. Let us discuss them with an open but morally sensitive mind, on as broad an international level as possible. And if we encounter

---

[21] However, things can get complicated, especially when it comes to the 'humanities' (cultural and social sciences), where interpretation plays an important role.

difficult issues such as the current one on embryonic stem-cell research, let us go on continuously evaluating the various and often opposing moral outlooks in order to find balanced answers and attitudes that take into account, as much as possible, the ethical values that are at stake.

A Catholic university can be an exquisite place to take the lead in the study of the relationship between science and faith and of the ethical limits to the basic freedom of research.

WHY WE ARE SO OBSESSED BY ISLAM?

Tariq Ali

Introduction by Ludo Abicht

In his book *Islam: Past, Present and Future* (2004), which is the final volume of a trilogy on the religions of the book – Judaism, Christianity and Islam – the German Catholic theologian and philosopher Hans Küng quotes Tariq Ali as an alternative voice on Islamic history and culture, as well as on the difficult interactions between today's leading civilizations. Küng raises the question: "Why didn't Islam, contrary to other world religions, such as Christianity and Judaism, witness a reformation? Why didn't we have renewal at that time? This reformation would have taken place if Islamic culture in al-Andalus had remained intact. However, the first large-scale ethnic cleansing in Europe happened in Spain, as we know, when Jews and Muslims were forced either to convert to Christianity or to leave the country. Europe was rebuilding its identity and did not care for the presence of foreigners".

None of the above is self-evident. Although both Hans Küng and Tariq Ali might be considered to be honourable dissenters against their own respective establishments, there is quite a difference between a devout Roman Catholic such as Hans Küng and a secular Muslim such as Tariq Ali. So why does Hans Küng, who after all is a world authority on religion, turn to a formal left-wing student activist, who, moreover, has ignored Winston Churchill's advice about the proper age for radicalism and conservatism and has remained an activist past the age of thirty. A modest answer to this rhetorical question would be: "Precisely because Tariq Ali has been able to keep the fires of moral indignation and hope for a better future burning, he is a credible discussion partner for Hans Küng and anyone else who cares to listen. I hope we are among those who care to listen to him."

Tariq Ali seems to imply that Islam, just like the other two monotheistic religions, ought to have had some form of reformation. Surely he knows that both orthodox Jews and traditionalist Roman Catholics would disagree with this statement. But this point of view is exactly the reason why Mr Ali has been invited to speak here among us, at the invitation of the University of Leuven, once a bastion of the Catholic counter-reformation. If the respectable University of Leuven can change and so to speak reform itself, then there is hope for the rest of the world. We know that both Christianity and Judaism have known a variety of different, at times mutually exclusive, forms of reformation. Therefore it will be crucial for Mr Ali to explain what kind of reformation he thinks will be necessary for the survival of Islam as a religion and a culture in the twenty-first century and maybe even beyond. Given the history of the Christian religion and the religious wars during the sixteenth and especially the seventeenth century (the famous Thirty Years' War), what does he propose for a genuine reformation that would avoid violent confrontations among the newly formed Muslim denominations, each of which will claim, as has generally happened with all religions, to be the legitimate heir to the legacy of the prophet? Mr Ali writes: "Why didn't we have a renewal at that time?"

Tariq Ali was born and spent his childhood in Lahore, now the capital of the western Punjab, a province of Pakistan. He studied at the University of Oxford and has lived and worked in London for most of his life. Politically, he is a devout internationalist and philosophically one could safely call him a non-dogmatic atheist. His novels, historical essays, television scripts, films, play and book reviews overall cover a wide variety of topics, from Marxist history and international working class movements to the condition of women in the Third World and the relationship between the Arab-Islamic world and western civilization. What, then, does he mean by "we" when he asks "why didn't 'we' have a renewal at that time?" After all, the postmodernist and politically correct new class is against any form of identity concept. However, Tariq Ali dares to talk about 'us'and 'we', implying there is a 'they'. If there is an 'us', there must be a 'they'. In his book on the current world situation, *The Clash of Fundamentalisms*, published in 2002, he acknowledges the existence of a number of major antagonistic forces, such as US imperialism and the international fundamentalist *Jihad*. But unlike Samuel Huntington and others, he's not convinced that the clash of civilizations is inevitable. Probable, yes, and possibly imminent if we are not careful, but not at all unavoidable.

Yet in spite of all his rational misgivings regarding the growth of Muslim and anti-Muslim fundamentalism, he does not abandon the culture of a tradition he happens to belong to by birth. Of course we all share the ethical and social duty to prevent this predicted and fatal clash of civilizations. But each of us also has a special obligation to take a long, hard and critical look at the developments within our own cultures and traditions. Thus to the key question, "why didn't 'we' experience a genuine reformation", 'we', that is to say this audience and myself, should add, "and what did 'we' do with the inheritance of our Reformation and, especially, of our celebrated Enlightenment?" That is not the topic of today's lecture, I know, but it is a problem we cannot walk away from in good faith.

As a keen student of history and a keen observer of his own time, Tariq Ali knows that the idea and practice of ethnic cleansing did not start with the *reconquista* in thirteenth-century Spain and that it is still going on in many areas of the world, where rulers and the manipulated masses of the people do not accept the presence of the other, of the foreigner. Neither does he lay the blame entirely on the intolerance of the Christians of the West, as he forcefully demonstrates in his book. But, it is a historical fact that the decline of the promising development of Arabic and Islamic philosophy coincided with the destruction of the unprecedented cultural richness of the Andalusian civilization to which Jewish and Christian scholars contributed alongside their Muslim colleagues, as you know. It is therefore interesting to note that Enlightenment philosophers, such as Voltaire with some notable exceptions, were the first to develop a serious interest in the achievements of non-Christian civilisations, Muslim, Arabic, as well as Chinese, and to start a lengthy, sometimes difficult process of re-evaluating the Arab-Muslim world that even today could help us to strengthen the necessary dialogue between proponents of different worldviews.

I am therefore confident that Tariq Ali, as a trained Marxist thinker, does not accept the various watered-down versions of these worldviews as a satisfactory answer, but is seriously committed to elaborating a kind of synthesis in which the constructive core elements of all major worldviews will gain from an open and honest confrontation, that certainly does not hide controversial issues but may bring us to a better mutual understanding of each other's and our own positions. It is therefore an honour and a pleasure now to turn the floor over to him.

Tariq Ali's Lecture

Introduction

Thank you very much for your kind words and to the organizers of these lectures for inviting me. To tell you the truth, I sometimes get quite fed up with this obsession with Islam. Why the obsession? Is it the case that Islam has suddenly become what it was once not? The answer is no. Or is it because the Islamo-anarchist terrorists who carried out the bombing raids of 9/11 happened to be Muslim, that this has now become a subject? I think the answer to the latter is yes.

Since 9/11 there has been a big change, and Islam has become an industry. More books have been published on Islam since 9/11 than ever before. You can just walk into a bookshop and can read the titles. Often a number of rather ignorant people who write books attacking Islam suddenly become celebrities and appear on one television station after the other. I find it slightly irritating. So what can we deduce from this, which is more universal and general? First, I think that since the collapse of the communist world, with all its defects and everything we know about what it stood for, there was a vacuum in the world. We were, if you like, going through a period of transition, but no one quite knew to what. Initially there was a lot of optimism: we would now live in a world without war, a world without need. Bush Sr. even began to talk about 'The Festive Event', combining a Kantian notion of peace with a more down-to-earth word: dividends. I think people stopped thinking for a long time. Many because they felt there was no alternative, no need to discuss anything: one side had triumphed in the Cold War and that was it. We could just carry on living our lives, shopping, enjoying celebrity culture, fornicating, etc., and that would be fine.

The comeback of religion: filling the vacuum

In this vacuum you saw the rise of religion globally. There was a definite increase in religiosity, let's call it that, throughout the whole world, not only the Islamic world. The country where religiosity has grown by leaps and bounds is a country that has always been more religious in my opinion than Europe, and that is the United States, where it had a very, very strong grip on the Republican Party through the new Christian right, Christian fundamentalism, born again Christians, etc.

This phenomenon is not limited to the United States. Although Europe – that is, Western Europe - is more secular, in Eastern Europe it has also seen a revival of religion, again because of the vacuum created with the fall of communism. Of course this rise of religion did not leave the Islamic world untouched, for it was experiencing a double vacuum: one created by the new world order, and one created by the policies of the Cold War, when the Islamists were the main allies of the United States in the struggle against secularists, nationalists, communists, socialists, in short anyone on the left. And you can look systematically at country after country in the Muslim world –Indonesia, Iran, Egypt, the Arab world – and see how adversely they were affected by the wiping out of all the alternatives.

This didn't happen everywhere at the same time, but by and large it took place over the last sixty years of the twentieth century. So the fact that there was no other alternative left in these countries made it obvious that the only doors that had been left open, very consciously, were the doors of the mosques. And the mosques would become the organizing centres for any movement that arose. That happened in Iran in the seventies, it happened in Saudi Arabia and produced al-Qaeda in the nineties, and it's happening in Pakistan even as we speak. The emergence of this vacuum in the nineties meant that something else had to appear, and unfortunately what appeared was religion, because there was nothing else in those parts of the world. In the West, especially the United States, the reason for the rise of religion is more variegated, but there too people felt that there was a vacuum, that the politics of either the Republicans or the Democrats did not really provide an answer to very deep spiritual needs.

This is a process we are even seeing in Europe right now, where differences between centre-left and centre-right have virtually been wiped out since the nineties. This leaves no real alternative with regard to the areas I mentioned. And it is this process that creates fragility and a disturbance in the world, rather than anything specifically to do with one religion. I think one has to try and see it that way, otherwise one falls into the Huntington trap, namely that we are now in the middle of a big clash of civilizations. Though to be fair to Samuel Huntington, he no longer holds that view. In what he has written since 9/11 he has said very clearly: "This is not what I meant, and in fact the clashes within civilizations are more dominant today." For him, the clash within Islam is the key issue.

This is a direct move, in other words, to discuss a political phenomenon in a religious language, trying to cover up any political differences by putting a religious mask on them, which has been going on for a very long time. Already in the 16th and 17th centuries, the wave of revolutions that took place in Europe wore religious masks. The English Revolution, for instance, can be interpreted in two different ways: Catholics would say it was a war of Protestant fundamentalism, which proved all the more successful under Cromwell and the Commonwealth. Others would say it was the struggle by the newly rising merchant layers in English society against the stranglehold of the monarchy and the feudal estates. In either case, there is no doubt that the ideology of the people leading the English revolution was hardcore Protestant fundamentalism, as was the ideology of the first settlers who arrived in the United States of America. And therefore you can even see a difference in the way in which South America and North America were colonized. But this simply means giving the process of revolution or colonization a religious mask.

Islam bridging between the ancient world and Europe

If we discuss the history of the three great monotheistic religions, Judaism, Christianity and Islam, in the order of their formation, it is not so dissimilar. Judaism and Islam in particular have quite a bit in common in the way in which they were formed: through clashes between tribes, through a desire to unify tribes, to have a unified ideology in the ancient world. Islam was lucky in the sense that it was the last of the three, so it could use quite a few ideas from both of the preceding religions. If you look at the *Qur'ân* it is filled with elements from the stories of the Old Testament, and its position on Jesus is to regard him as a great saint. It does not accept, which is more rational, that he was the son of God, and it challenges the virgin birth, quite correctly as we now know.

But between the seventh and the eleventh centuries, so for four hundred years, Islamic civilization was the bridge between the learning of the ancient world and Europe, and later these ideas were to fuel the Renaissance. It is now well known that most of the texts of the ancient world were translated by a school of translators sitting in Tolaitola, now known as Toledo, the largest translation centre of the early medieval world, translating all the Greek texts they had found into Arabic, and then from Arabic into Latin. So we know that these worlds were very closely interrelated and linked.

The notion that Islam is intrinsically hostile to ideas of democracy is not true. I think that in order to understand what Islam is, one has to stop talking about a single Islam as a stereotype. Think of a palette on which painters put all the colours they are going to use – I would suggest that Islam, like Christianity and to a lesser extent Judaism (because that is a far more closed religion), has many different colours on its palette. The reason for this is very simple. You cannot understand Islam without understanding the speed with which it spread. That is what distinguishes it from Christianity. Christianity took a long time to grow, and it grew in the course of a long struggle against the Roman Empire, emerging in the cracks and flaws of that Empire, until finally it took over the Empire when the latter needed a strong ideology in its declining days, as Edward Gibbon, the great English historian of the Roman Empire describes very well.

Islam on the other hand, grew very rapidly, and the reason it did so was that the two empires surrounding it were already in the process of disintegrating. The great Zoroastrian empire of the Persians and the Byzantine Empire based in Constantinople were in decline, and this coincided with the rise of this tribal confederation that became Islam, which was led - unfortunately for its own future – by extremely gifted political and military leaders. That is how I look at them, because since I am not religious myself, one has to look at these events historically: what they were, how they came about, etc. Otherwise you cannot understand how, within a hundred years of its birth, Islam had already reached China, brought by traders, and had also expanded to the shores of the Atlantic, in Spain and Portugal. Soon the Persian Empire fell, Byzantium began to break up, and all their territories were taken over by this new political movement, religion, whatever you want to call it.

The result was that Islam had to invent theory and ideology and religious practice on the move. For if you look at the *Qur'ân*, although it contains a great many things, there is very little in it that can give you what devout Muslims call "a complete code of life". It is not a complete code of life. So things had to be invented, and virtually the bulk of Islamic practice and tradition was invented long after Mohammed's death and long after the first *Qur'ân* was compiled. And hence there is in Islamic history a set of precepts known as traditions, Hadiths, which supposedly were uttered by the prophet of Islam, or by people very close to him. In reality, most of them were in fact invented. Invented to serve the needs of this new, rapidly growing religious empire which had emerged from nowhere, on the Arabian Peninsula, and was spreading everywhere. From the very beginning, because it didn't have a clear-cut way of approaching the world, it split. It was divided.

The father of history, Ibn al Hadum, who more or less invented history as a scientific subject in the Middle Ages, wrote extremely far-sightedly that the big problem with Islam was that it never understood the concept of solidarity. And that it was always clashing within itself. So it is not simply the case that they lost Andalusia (which comprised Spain and Portugal and Sicily) because the Christian offensive was all that powerful or militarily superior; that was partly the case, but they also lost because they did not have a sense of Islam as a unified cultural civilization. By the time Islam moved to Europe there were three Caliphs, not one. One in Baghdad, one in Cairo and one in Córdoba. Each ruled in a different way, each had completely different traditions.

And the reason Andalusia and the Iberian peninsula is talked about more than the other two is that this is where Islam coexisted for 400-500 years with Christianity and Judaism, and this coexistence produced one of the most wonderful civilizations. We should not exaggerate; it was wonderful compared to the present. And within this civilization you had Jewish and Christian and Muslim philosophers debating, discussing, fighting each other all the time with words, with documents, and that improves everyone. It raises the level of an entire civilization when that happens, and that did happen. Some amazing texts and documents and books were produced during that period. Many of them, though not all, fortunately, were burnt in a great fire in December 1499, on the orders of the Inquisition to burn all the Muslim books in Grenada. A lot disappeared there, but much survived, so we know a bit about that civilization.

Looked at from this perspective, we come to the question: why was there no reformation in Islam? And I think that is why. Islam was forcibly pushed out of Europe, out of both Sicily and Spain, in quite a brutal way. It never recovered, and it is significant that while in Europe great technological gains took place from at least the eighteenth century, culminating in the Industrial Revolution, Islam was already absent from the European continent. It had been ghettoized, and there it would remain.

Contradictory aspects about Islam

If it were not for a theological and geographical accident, namely that the bulk of the world's cheap oil today lies beneath Islamic lands, would anyone even be discussing Islam? Probably not, or it would be seen as just another esoteric Eastern religion like Buddhism or Hinduism or Jainism. Now, let's put forward a counterfactual argument, let's say that all the rich oil-producing countries from Brunei to the Middle East, the Arabian Peninsula, Iran, etc. were Buddhist. Would we not see a massive industry in Buddhism? Especially if a handful of Buddhists had attacked the US. That's what would have happened, and that is what gives Islam its importance, there is no other reason, in my opinion. It is the oil and the enormous richness that make that region absolutely crucial. Without that, what is it? Islam is a religion like any other, and it would survive probably for some time, but it is the oil wealth that gives it its importance, and the money available from it permits many exhibitions to be held and museums to be built about Islamic civilization and culture. This is wonderful, but at the same time the wealth permits the Saudi Arabian government to buy off most of the academic departments in the United States, so you can't get any critical books on Saudi Arabia coming out of the American academies. That is a problem which money can create.

Thus there are many, many contradictory aspects to Islam. What are the solutions? Reformation? Well, a reformation can only come from within a country, if there is to be a proper reformation. It is not going to come with foreign occupations and armies. Young people, especially today, often forget that the West has a colonial past. Mainly Europe, with the United States coming after the Second World War. But the European record of colonialism is not a particularly good one. Even if you consider the people who are proclaimed as the most enlightened colonialists, the British, it is an awful record. They spent 150 years in India, and when they left, 90% of the population was still illiterate, and nearly 60% was suffering from malnutrition in one form or the other, so it's not exactly a brilliant record. The notion of a new colonialism in the modern world, with fancy new language, somehow means going into that world to transform and modernise it. It is exploding in front of our eyes every single day in Iraq. One reason it is exploding is that the people who live in that part of the world do not have the luxury of forgetting their history. Europeans forget their history. If I were them, I would want to forget quite a lot of it as well. But the people who live in that part of the world can't and don't forget it, because they know what happened and why.

So it's very difficult to understand that world without understanding what has happened in the past, which is why they talk so much about history. The clashes that we see today are thus a clash with a great power, the United States of America – the only imperial power left in the world, I would argue, even if its imperialism takes a very different form from that of the Europeans, in the sense that by and large the United States did not like occupying countries but preferred finding people locally who could run them on their behalf: you save money, you save lives and you still have the country. And this is still what the Americans do: Iraq is occupied, but the rest of the Arab world isn't directly occupied, though they are large US military bases. Saudi Arabia is run by the Saudi royal family, which was elevated to the status of royalty by the British Empire and then had that status guaranteed by the United States after the Second World War.

The fact that these have been stealing wealth and money from their country for the last sixty years no one likes to talk about, because they do have the money. But that is a country totally in the pocket of the

United States. It has a very small army and air force, but spends more on defence than many countries twenty times its size. So where are all these planes and latest weaponry? They are all in warehouses in the desert, rotting. They have to buy them, because that is part of the deal, but they do not dare to create a large army, because they are afraid that it might overthrow the monarchy. So these are some of the interesting contradictions, which have nothing to do with religion and everything to do with economics and the way the world is run and organized.

If you look at Islam as a very large palette with different colours, then you can see it more clearly. There is no one Islam, even if we leave aside the Shia and the Sunni. Because of the speed with which Islam took these countries, it had to negotiate with the local cultures and religions and incorporate a lot of their elements. For instance, Islam in the Indian subcontinent owes a great deal to local tradition, which doesn't come from the Arab world. The largest Muslim country in the world, Indonesia, took over a number of pagan and Hindu customs that already existed in that country. As just one example, one thing forbidden explicitly in the *Qur'ân* and punishable by death is male homosexuality. Not female homosexuality, but male homosexuality, because that threatens everything. But culturally, Indonesia is virtually 99% bisexual – that is how it always was. The greatest works of Indonesian literature are centred on homosexuality. So was Islam able to wipe it out? Far from it, it is still exactly the same, and the first gay movie in the Muslim world, in which an architect comes out as gay, was shown in Indonesia about two and a half years ago. Did the clergy come forward and demonstrate that this was a breach of the Sharia and the *Qur'ân*? No, because they knew it would be foolish to do so, because probably half or three-quarters of the clergy are gay themselves.

So you have this contradiction that there is no easily available stereotype. And Chinese Islam, which is quite large, with millions of Muslims in China but totally 'Chinafied', if you like, picking up a lot from that culture. So ultimately the point is that when in the West people talk about Islam, what they really mean is the rich oil-producing countries. They're not interested in the rest, where a large majority of Muslims actually live in the world and lead their daily lives. It is all about the oil, about who is going to have control of that wretched oil. And that is what determines these attitudes.

Islam in Europe

The third point I want to make is that what has changed gradually over the last thirty or forty years, maybe even longer, I suppose, is that for the first time in Europe now, since the Middle Ages, you have a large Muslim population in Europe, between 15 and 20 million spread all over Europe. This is new. And this phenomenon is very different from that of ancient or medieval civilization, because these are not people who rule countries but who are in many cases on the lowest rung of the ladder and perform menial work, migrant labour. This is creating cultural problems, disputes, which is quite normal. Whenever you have large-scale migration, in my opinion it takes at least 30 to 40 years for integration to begin. This is true of the United States as well, which is the country to which migrants came from all over Europe, but it took some time for them to settle in. The Irish, who were the last massive wave of migrants, faced a lot of hostility, just as there was a lot of hostility towards the Irish who migrated to Britain during the famine. It is astonishing to see what was written about them. In many cases they were referred to, especially in the Liverpool region, as 'green niggers', which is an interesting phenomenon. It sums up how people thought of them - they were the outsiders. It took them a long time to integrate, and I think that will be the same in the case of Muslims, provided some things add up.

Now poor people tend to search for an identity that can help them fight the wealthy, who they feel have been unfair to them. This, too, goes back to the ancient world. Many similar disputes and discussions took place in the ancient world as well, although in different ways, of course, because the populations were much smaller. The questions which arise are therefore the following: should we take a relativist attitude and say that because a minority belongs to a certain religion, the community should have the right to treat its people on the basis of something that the clergy have decided are its religious texts? Once you start down that road, there is no end, because if even when talking only about Islam, you have multiple interpretations.

Take, for instance, temporary marriages of convenience, to use a polite word for it, which means if a man decides he wants to sleep with a woman, he can get a certificate from the clergy (of course women cannot get such a certificate) after having paid some money, and depending on how much he has paid, he can then sleep with her for one, two or three nights, and it is recognised as a temporary marriage of convenience. Everywhere in the world this just happens, yet that is not permissible within Sunni Islam, which is the majority within Islam. Now they, too, are looking for similar rules, because why should the Shia have a moral advantage, so to speak.

Therefore as far as Europe today is concerned, I am in favour of having one set of laws for the entire population, even though some members of the Islamic community are angry with me for saying so. No concessions on this should be made. That the areas where problems arise are those where there are no reformation values in place. In Spain, for instance, the Catholic Church controls the education system. Now if you want to deny Muslims the right to open Islamic madrassas, then you have to have an education system, which is the same for everyone, you cannot grant Christians and Jews the right to open their own schools but deny that right to another section of the population.

This ought to compel the leadership of the European Union to move in that direction, but so far it has not been doing so. Tony Blair in Britain, in particular, strongly encouraged single-faith schools because he is himself a religious believer. This is something that few people know about him, but he is quite definite in this area and encouraged the creation of single-faith schools because he says that the community knows best how to educate its own children. However, we are not talking about communities here, but about the clergy, the church, the synagogue and the mosque having control over education. I don't think that's a good thing, either for the kids who are being educated or for the country as a whole.

A single education system is extremely important. I'm indeed in favour of a single education system, but not of having a big fight over what women wear on their heads provided they want to wear it, or whether Jews should be allowed to wear a skullcap. If women want to wear the hijab, it's their right to do so, and it is important to take that position if we are opposed to the state imposing this on women. In Saudi Arabia, in Iran, and so on, women are not allowed to go out without their head covering; we oppose that and say it is wrong. Well, it's equally wrong to say to women: "you can't do it". You can't have one without the other. So one has to approach the question with care, because it is a foolish fight, this fight over the headscarf. It gives a reason to the wrong people within the Muslim community to say: "we're being totally isolated, see, we aren't even allowed to do this". They will use this argument, so it is foolish to prohibit it.

As regards the educational and legal system that prevails in a country, however, we have to be very firm, there is one category that we recognize, and that is known as citizenship. All citizens are equal before this law and all citizens have the same rights. Where this is not the case, or where there is no separation of church and state – as there isn't in Britain or in Spain, then there are big problems. You cannot then deny one section of the population their rights. The second question that arises, which I referred to earlier, is that of integration. This is not going to happen overnight. It takes time – three or four generations – and then integration takes often place in ways people don't like.

For instance, I was being interviewed on French radio and television at the time of the riots in France, when the North African kids rioted after the police had chased two of them, and one of them had died. And I said to the French journalists: "I know you're not going to like this, but the way these kids react shows that they're integrated. They built barricades, they attacked property, and they set cars on fire. Isn't that very French? 1789, 1848, 1871, 1968, and so on. You have a pattern, and they've absorbed French history better than you imagine." And then, two weeks after that, French students did the same thing, white French students, some of whose privileges were being threatened, did exactly the same thing on the streets, and there was no Sarkozy to call them barbarians or savages. They did exactly the same thing, they fought on the streets, just showing, proving the point I was making.

It would not happen in the same way in Britain, because the traditions there are different, and it would not take the same form in Germany, because the traditions in Germany are different as well. But young people growing up in these societies do take in, in different ways, some of the culture and history of the country in which they live. Often I hear young Islamists in Britain using arguments that were used by the leaders of the Labour Party fifty years ago, and saying "we are being denied these things". It is very interesting how that works. There is no automatic, linear way in which this integration will take place, but that is what people want integration to be.

Of course, as I have always believed, integration is not simply related to skin colour or religion, but is also very closely related to class. It is perfectly possible for a multi-millionaire from any part of the Muslim world to have no problems at all with integration because he lives a life in which he barely comes in contact with the real world, so he is totally integrated. This is true even today. That is to say, I don't think the Arab elite have any problems being integrated in London or Paris or anywhere else. They are integrated and are treated extremely well. These problems arise by and large only for people who have very little money, and who for whatever reason feel they are being treated unfairly by the state in the particular country they live in. They then begin to develop a form of identity politics, which in recent years has taken the form of religion, whereas previously it might have taken the form of race.

Using religion as the basis for identity is very new, by the way, amongst migrant communities in Europe. The first wave of migrants who came did not use it but tried to integrate. However, the large South Asian and West Indian populations that came to Britain integrated very well. They tried to join the big trade unions and the local political parties, but in many cases they were not permitted to integrate. In other cases they were integrating so well that the state encouraged preachers to come in from their countries of origin to tell them they should be going to the pub less and attending the mosque more. So it's a very complicated and complex story, which we can't get away from.

Anger at the West

Essentially what I would really advise against is treating Islam as a stereotype. There is opposition to what the United States has done in Iraq, there is great opposition to what is going on in Palestine, but this opposition in Palestine has been going on for nearly forty years. One of the problems is the double standard employed by the West, especially in relation to Palestine. That is why it hurts and it runs very deep, not just among religious Muslims, but even among secular people in that culture. The fact that the West has ignored the suffering of the Palestinians, that the great, much- touted Western liberal conscience is blind when it comes to Palestinian suffering. The reason for that is directly related to the Judeocide that took place during the Second World War all over Europe. Yet the Palestinians were not the perpetrators of the Judeocide, they simply become its indirect victims. we are a long way from that now, crimes are committed in this world, horrible crimes. Crimes were committed in the colonial epoch, by the French in Algeria, the British in India, the Belgians in the Congo. But you cannot blame the Belgian people of today for those crimes, this is a totally different generation! So why blame the Europeans of today for the crimes of Judeocide, which were horrible crimes as we all know. How long is this going to be used as blackmail, because the effect that it has on the Arab world is fatal.

People were prepared to overthrow Milosevic in the Balkans, 2000 people died in Kosovo. Yet how many are dying in Palestine every single month? And how many young people are dying? And how many are dying in Iraq, and you don't open your mouths! That is the big problem, and this applies to the three kids who did this horrible thing in London a few years ago on July 7th, blew themselves up and planted bombs. One of their people was caught in Italy, and Italian interrogators asked him "why did you do it? You know, while you're studying the *Qur'ân*, did the *Qur'ân* teach you to do this?" And the guy laughed in his face and said: "don't be stupid! What do you think? We were reading the *Qur'ân* day in and day out? We were watching videotapes of what the Americans had done in Fallujah, with help from Blair, and we wanted to punish Blair". And every single British institute now, including the Institute for International Relations, and numerous other official think-tanks that have researched this, have come up with the same answer, that it was British foreign policy and not religion that was responsible. After all, if it had been religion, why not bomb Paris, Berlin, Brussels? It was a direct attack, for a particularly wrong; it was unjustifiable carnage, but you have to understand the causes, because unless the causes are understood, these events will continue to happen.

Within the Arab world there is another very deep anger at the West for having tolerated these corrupt regimes for too long. If you look at Osama bin Laden's videotapes, the ones he made long before 9/11 and distributed within Saudi Arabia (I watched them because I was working on them for my book), they are actually very consistent. What he says is: "our country's oil wealth is being stolen by this one family, this family has been given the franchise to run Saudi Arabia by the British and then by the United States, and this money is not being spent for the welfare of our people or our region". He then cites the names of princes of the royal family whom he knows very well, and says: "shall I tell you where Prince X will be even as you're watching this? He'll be in a casino in Monaco, losing half a million dollars in one night. That is where Prince Z will be: in a casino in Monte Carlo", and he just names them and the amount of money they lose each week at the gaming tables. So you can just imagine how effective it is, because it is true. The religious stuff is completely different, of course, it is a combination of fantasy and craziness, but it is the former that wins him support. We do not need tougher laws against women, that is not what gets him the support, it is this point that gets him the support.

So this is the reality in the world today, and it is much better, I argue, to allow elections in these countries, to permit some form of democracy to function, so that people know they can remove a government when they want to. That is healthy. In Egypt, what would it mean if this happened? It would mean that the Islamists, the Muslim Brotherhood, would probably win between 30 and 40 percent of the votes. Who are these people? If you talk to them, they sound like European Christian

Democrats, and that is what they are. They are socially conservative, but otherwise they are no different. They have a different religion, and they are very similar to the people in power in Turkey today, who are also Christian Democrats, but of an Islamist variety. So what is the point of backing Hosni Mubarak by spending billions on this corrupt, motheaten dictatorship each year? It is a pointless exercise, one that helps no one, and Egypt does not even have any oil. At least in Saudi Arabia you want your own contractors to look out for the oil, but in Egypt there is no oil, it is just a powerful old civilisation.

Conclusion

I always argue that unfortunately for those of us who write books, the best teacher of a population is not books, because most people do not read books, but rather their own experience. The best way people will learn whether the Islamists are doing right or wrong is if they are in power. There is no other way to do it. Turkey is now engaged in this debate. When the Islamists tried to change a law slightly – not too much, only slightly – half a million people marched in Istanbul in support of the secular traditions of the Turkish state. The same thing would happen in Egypt if democracy were permitted. Likewise in the Maghreb. So this is the world in which we live, it is a complex world, there are no easy solutions, but there are right ways and wrong ways of doing things, and unfortunately since 9/11 the regime in Washington has done things wrong, as even its own people realise. And by the way that is something that should not be underestimated – when people in the Arab world see Americans demonstrate against the war in Iraq, they have two immediate reactions: "God, we have a few friends there!" and "They're allowed to demonstrate against their own country...". So it has a double impact.

The present situation is bad. I think it could even get worse. For instance if Iraq breaks up, or Turkey invades northern Iraq in pursuit of the Kurds, which is not totally impossible, the situation could get much worse than we can even imagine. The worst would be if there was any foolishness in relation to Iran. I don't think there will be because although this is never openly discussed, without the support of Iran, the United States could neither have taken Iraq or Afghanistan. The Iranian Mullahs agreed to it for reasons of their own, each State acting in its own interest. The Iranians wanted to get rid of Saddam for their own reasons, so they backed the Americans, and they wanted to get rid of the Taliban for their own reasons, so they backed the Americans. So this notion of some deep fundamental clash between the Iranians and the United states is a joke, it does not exist on that level. But what it does mean is that if any craziness is done in relation to Iran, you will have war on three fronts simultaneously: Iran, Afghanistan and Iraq. If the Iranians decide to go that way, they can end these occupations. And I think the Pentagon, which is often more intelligent than the politicians in power, knows that very well. This is why there was so much hostility at the Pentagon to the war in Iraq in the first place, because they knew what they were getting into.

As far as Europe is concerned, what is needed is time, time and consistency, and no double standards. There is no big problem concerning Islam as such, and one should not use acts carried out by tiny minorities to stigmatise that culture as a whole any more than one would have regarded the anarchists who brought Europe to a standstill in the 19th and early 20th centuries as a reflection on Christian culture and civilization. What the anarchists did in virtually every major European country was not so dissimilar: killing civilians, blowing up heads of state, and it was a very similar sort of people who did these things, although with a different purpose.

Questions and Answers

Q. Why don't a number of religious Islamic leaders speak out more clearly, the way you do, namely, that things should not be perpetrated in the name of religion?

A. Because they're religious leaders. They're religious leaders, and their so-called prestige is built on defending their religion. And that is what Tony Blair is doing, and what the French are trying to do – to create their own group of religious leaders who will speak on their behalf. The problem is, this is not going to work. Often these religious leaders are people who run to the mosques and say that they are leaders of the religious community, and the governments accept them as such. One of the problems is that there are no elections, you don't know who these religious leaders are, or who has appointed them. And some of the young kids who go crazy do so precisely because of these religious leaders. I can think of hardly a single religious leader in Europe who is respected, actually, even within the community, let alone outside it. For instance, a few years ago Sarkozy was debating Tariq Ramadan when in one state in eastern Nigeria the religious leader said that they should institute Islamic punishment for adultery and theft – which is stoning to death and chopping off hands (there was a big debate as to whether you chop the hand at the wrist, or just the fingers, but we won't go into this detail today). And Sarkozy asked Tariq Ramadan: "what would you say to these Nigerian people?" And instead of replying: "I would tell them to stop this nonsense, etc., etc.", he said: "I would ask them to consider a moratorium". That is the scale of the problem.

Q. You said that you are in favour of one set of laws for the entire population, and you combine that with the idea of a single education system. Would that mean, then, that some European constitutions should be changed with regard to freedom of education, that we should abandon several of our fundamental liberties in order to elaborate a consistent system of education?

A. What liberties would you abandon?

Q. One of the liberties in many countries, and also in certain constitutions, is freedom of education, and that's a principle that also includes the right to organize education, provided you comply with certain standards. So what would your attitude be with regard to that freedom?

A. My attitude would be that there should be a total separation between State and religion on every level, including education; however, if the religious groups want special education, then they can provide it on the weekend, like you used to have and still have some special weekend schools and Sunday schools, and best of luck to them. But if the State education system is really to be cut off from religion, and if that requires a change of constitution, this should happen.

Q. *I'm not focusing on Sunday schools and religious education as such, but what you see in many countries is that when free enterprise is able to organize education and complies with objective standards, set forward by the authorities, then it's fine, even if those suppliers of education are a Muslim or a Catholic or whatever organisation. And if I can add something to that, you were also insisting on complete separation between Church and State, and you were quoting the examples of Spain and the UK, where that complete separation is not achieved. But as a matter of fact, it doesn't exist in any European country. Even in countries like France, where, let's say, there is quite a severe form of separation, we see that chaplains are financed, that there are contracts between religious schools and the State, that even Sarkozy was very unhappy that he had to deal with all this just in order to organize a dialogue with religious people. I mean, complete separation, is it not an illusion?*

A. I can see your point. My position is that religion is going to be here for a long time. I don't think it is going to disappear. People have a perfect right to believe in whatever they want, but in States that are multicultural and multireligious, should the State – or private enterprise, for that matter – put forward religious schools under whatever guise? Personally I'm not in favour of it, but all I'm saying is, it's up to you. I don't like it, but if you want it to stay like that then you can't stop having Muslim aggressors in Europe. You can't have it both ways.

Q. *But to me it comes down to a very fundamental point. On the one hand you are pleading, and rightly so, in my view, in favour of one law for everybody, but that could also mean that that law is adapted, given the new inhabitants of Europe, and that could even imply a* *change with regard to fundamental rights. That is not an innocent proposal.*

A. No, it isn't an innocent proposal. But it is quite a serious one, and I'll tell you why, because this debate goes on in Pakistan, where you have a lot of Madrassas. Though I grant that it's very different from Europe, but still, the principle is not so different. There you don't have a State educational system worthy of the name, it doesn't exist, and so you have two different forms of education in Pakistan: one is a Western style education for those who are well off, middle class or rich, where the medium of instruction is English, where the teachers are of a good standard, and where increasingly foreign universities set up bases for a tiny, tiny minority of the population. Then you have the religious Madrassas, which are set up by various factions - most of them are Wahhabi Madrassas, and they say to poor families: "your family is poor, you have six children, we will educate your kids for free. We'll feed them, clothe them, educate them". Basically these schools have become nurseries for the *Jihad*, there's no big secret about it. And for me that is the debate, which colours my attitude generally as well, I have to admit. These schools should all be closed down and the millions and millions and millions in funding coming from the EU and America to back this regime should insist on setting up a State education system, where, as the Malaysians have already done, English becomes a compulsory language for everyone, giving people more access to a different literature that is currently not available. So that's my attitude, I'm totally opposed to the Madrassas. And even in Europe, I think it's in the interest of the European Union to try to create an education system which is uniform. I'm not in favour of totally crushing all independent initiatives, far from it, but I think the principles have to be uniform. Very rich people, Muslim millionaires, will happily set up schools of the sort you're talking about, and even say that the standards are very good. But we know what goes on, and we know what sort of teachers would be involved. For instance, for a start, would they be co-educational schools? And I'm prepared to bet you that most of them wouldn't. You know, I'm not even opposed to single-sex schools in some cases, it could be useful to have them, but here the hostility to co-education is institutionalized. So I'm saying that it becomes difficult now, with 16 to 20 million people (in Europe) belonging to a totally different religion. If there's one law already in existence permitting religious schools, or private religious schools, funded by churches or whatever, but then denying that right to the Muslim population, it would be much better to have a uniform system. Better for Europe and better for the citizens who are to be produced, and better for integration at some level.

Q. *If education is really important, how do you empower women? How do you educate people?*

A. A very important question. When I speak of education I just take it for granted that you understand I mean the education of everyone, not just young men. Surveys that have been done, interestingly, even in one of what is supposedly the most backward areas of Pakistan, precisely in the border regions, show that when the questions are properly framed and families or fathers are asked: "would you like your daughters to be educated?", a majority replies: "yes!". But they don't want them to be educated in co-educational schools. Setting up groups, training teachers, women teachers, to teach in these schools and educate young girls is absolutely vital. There are few independent groups that have done it with some success without any State support at all in these backward areas. I know this very well because my sister is an educationalist, and this is what she has been concerned with for the last twenty years of her life. She has actually helped to set up these schools, train teachers, send them in, and they have been relatively successful. Of course there are not many of them, five or six, but what it shows is that if the State were really determined it could do it. Why would it be stopped by fundamentalists? And if it is, then you deal with them, and say that this is a right of women. Where does it say anywhere in Islam that you don't educate women? These are by and large old tribal traditions. Islam has been added on to them. It's something a strong government would be perfectly capable of doing and should do. And not just there, but all over the Muslim world.

Q. *You mention the figure of 15 to 20 million Muslims in Europe, which is certainly the figure that is generally agreed, but that's 15 or 20 million out of 450 or 500 million Europeans, so in reality it is not that great. I think that the Americans who these days say: "Europe is becoming Eurabia" are completely exaggerating the situation. The problem, I think, arises because most of these Muslims are concentrated into small areas of very large cities and the social tensions arise out of that. Do you think there's any remedy for that, or is that something we just have to live with?*

A. I agree with you entirely. It is historically important that on a continent where Muslims were once part of the landscape, and which was ethnically cleansed, Muslims are once again part of the landscape after so many centuries. This should be normal, but one reason it isn't normal is that there is no sense of history or of what happened in the past. But of course you're absolutely right, it's nothing compared to the overall population of Europe, and you're right again that the reason for the ghettoization is largely socio-economic tensions and the fact that they belong to the poorer sections of the community. It has always been thus, and there was a very interesting study done in Britain by an academic – I can't remember her name – who researched all the things that were being said in London about Jewish migrants who came and settled in the East End after three waves of pogroms in Poland and Russia. She quoted from what was said about the Jews at the time, and it's virtually the same as what is being said about the Muslims in Europe today: they don't integrate, they smell, no one says that too loudly today, but many people feel it, they eat funny food and so on. And worse: they have long hair, etc. It's just astonishing what was being said. So nothing changes, new migrants come in, in 40-50 years, and similar things are beginning to be said about the Poles today, by the way, in parts of Europe, because you have a massive migration from Eastern Europe, and Poland in particular, to many countries, including Britain. And some of this language is being used about the Poles. This has got nothing to do with religion or skin colour. So there is a logic, an awful, twisted logic in the way migrants are treated when they come basically to find work.

One of the ironies is that we live in a world where the Washington consensus on liberal economics is absolutely settled; no politician, in Europe certainly, breaks with it, but without understanding fully the consequences of this for their own societies and their own countries. This is a system where you say that capital can go anywhere, but labour can't, and those capital flows are basically denuding the Third World of what it used to have, and the new laws about reducing the role of the state all over the world and the entry of private capital in what used to be considered the hallowed domains of social provision, all that is going. The effect of that even in Europe can be bad, and in Britain it is bad, as we see in parts of the country, but in Africa and in parts of Asia it's devastating. And if China follows the WTO rules, in the next five years there could be at least twenty to thirty million Chinese out of work, and then where will they go? They would go to where they can find jobs, which is why people always leave a country. There's an economic crisis, there's a famine, there's no work, that's why Germans and Irish and English and others left and found the New World. They didn't particularly want to go, but they had no option. The world hasn't changed in that regard, it's just that the balance has shifted, so people go where they can find work. And one answer to the solution is to create and permit a better social and economic system, which doesn't make them want to leave their own country, but to say this in today's world is heresy. Almost as bad as religious heresy.

Q. You said in the beginning that since the end of the Cold War, religion is on the rise, but the more I read about it, the more I have the impression that religion was already on the rise before the end of the Cold War. It was a reaction against the values of modernity or postmodernity, and in Middle Eastern and North African countries against the regimes which incorporated those western values, so that it was already present before, also in India and in the United States, with the evangelical movements, etc. But with the end of the Cold War, once international politics was no longer preoccupying people's minds, religion simply became more visible. People began to identify more on the basis of religion, which is possible because people are labelling them by their religion. I think it's remarkable that here in Europe people now speak of Muslims, and no longer of the Turks, Moroccans, Pakistanis, etc. I just wonder why that's happened?

A. Well, it's true that there was an increase in religion, even before the Cold War formally came to an end, but I would say that this began to happen really in a big way, leaving aside the Iranian developments, which were very specific. At the time of the Iranian Revolution of the '70s, in '78-'79, there was no guarantee that the clerics would take over, but they did, and one reason they did was because the non-clerical people made a lot of mistakes as well. But it's true that the clerics were strong because, as I explained earlier, the mosques were the organizing centres because these was nothing else. It was the same, to an extent, in Poland, where the churches were the organizing centres. In every authoritarian society, where people have nowhere else to meet, they go to what's open. If you can't talk in cafés because they're packed with secret police agents, you go to church. So in Poland you had the church playing a great part in the Solidarnosc movement, but it was very political. What has happened subsequent to the Cold War is a slightly different phenomenon, not totally unrelated to it, but different from it, which is that there was a great sense that no alternatives were possible. That is also beginning to change now, by the way, but for twenty years we've had a pretty big vacuum.

The last part of your question was that people now refer to Muslims rather than to Moroccans, Maghrebis, Pakistanis, etc. I think that's the 9/11 effect. You can link it very, very clearly to that event; that is when the decision was made that the new enemy is Islam. However, it's foolish, because there are so many differences, which I've explained, within the Islamic communities, and one big problem is also that the different states in Europe tend to go for religious leaders to represent these communities. Why? It's not that everyone is a religious person within these communities – there are lots of secular people, but they're never encouraged, and that also worries me. Britain is a bad example in this case, but the French are doing the same thing, saying: "we are training our own imams", etc., where is this going to end?

Q. Somewhere in one of the articles you warn us not to have too homogeneous a view of Islam. Islam is, you are right, a palette of ideological positions. What we see in Europe is the potential for identification with Islam, which offers a kind of market of identities to youngsters. What can we do as a majority society and host society to facilitate, without being too paternalistic, this kind of search for identity among young Muslims? Is there a responsibility on part of the public authorities? Maybe we were looking too much for religious leaders, who are not necessarily the leaders of the community. What can a majority society do in terms of facilitating a type of identification, but leaving it to the youngsters which ideological position is theirs?

A. There are big divisions along political lines, sometimes along religious lines, and I think one has just got to understand that over the next twenty to thirty years, depending on what happens to these societies, you will have large numbers of migrants who will participate in the different institutions of these societies, as they already do in the United States to a certain extent, but also in Britain. Whatever else can be said, Britain has members of Parliament, leaders of trade unions who come from migrant communities and have been integrated. What you need are deep-going social and economic reforms to reduce or end the condition of the lowest level of strata in society, which these migrants are, whether they are Muslims or non-Muslims. And that seems very unlikely, given the way the world is going and given increasingly what is happening to this world, and what is also worrying. The figures from Britain show that this sense of alienation doesn't simply affect tiny minorities of migrants, or recent migrants or their families, but in the last two general elections in Britain, a majority of young people between the ages of 18 and 26 did not vote. They just didn't vote. In France it is different, you had a very high level of voting, with about three million voters from the most depressed areas coming in and voting, to try and keep Sarkozy out, but whether this is something which is permanent or something more conjunctural, we don't know. So it depends, there's no easy answer, and each country has its own different traditions, but I think a big start would be to end the stereotyping. That would help. Not about all Muslims, just as one doesn't do about Christians.

Q. *I would like to go back for a minute to your one universal set of laws, of educational principles. Many people argue here as well as in other European countries, and outside, that our values are universal values. But they are basically European values that we are imposing on others. In other words, it's a new form of soft colonialism. And many Europeans, non-migrant Europeans, who call themselves "cultural relativists" and believe in the equality of all values, agree with them. So what do you answer to them? They're saying these universal values that you would teach at those schools are basically imposing in an unarmed way, in a non-military way, our European values upon non-Europeans.*

A. I don't agree with that. I know that this argument is put forward, especially by postmodernists, but it's an argument I have criticized. What it boils down to actually is leaving people in their ghettos in the name of postmodernist relativism, and it's not helpful. It's not helpful in the academy either, by the way, but it's certainly not helpful in society as a whole. Everyone knows what the conditions are in which the migrants live, and you know, lots of people, after the riots in France, did detailed surveys, and what these surveys showed was so widespread that even President Chirac had to acknowledge it and say "we have to do something". They showed that these young kids go into a French school, a normal school in most cases, and that school teaches them that once they leave school, they will be

French citizens, they will have equality before the law, they will have the same opportunities, etc. All the values of the French Republic. But when they leave these schools, they find that the reality is very different from what they were promised at school, and Chirac said – and it's astonishing for a conservative president to say this – Chirac actually said that he was shocked when he read these reports, and he said there is a colour bar which operates in France, though, as we know, not on the football field. People are not given jobs simply because of their skin colour. It's a deep-rooted problem, but its solution is not relativism, or saying: "you educate your own people, you know them best", that's basically copping out.

Q. Listening to you and reading you, it's clear that you are a believer in the ideas of the Enlightenment and that you are against postmodern multiculturalism. And yet I have not received, and I'm curious to hear, your answer to Ludo Abicht's question in his presentation, where he asked you: "why do you keep saying 'we'?", because that seems indeed rather contradictory to the universalistic view that you have so eloquently exposed.

A. It's obvious why I said "we", because I'm appealing to a layer of young people within the Muslim community, who come to my meetings, talk with me, speak with me, so it's a way of identifying with some of their problems, obviously, that's the reason why I said "we". The one thing I want you to know is this: I speak a lot to meetings of young Muslims, who know I'm not a believer. They even know I'm an atheist, because it's spelt out very openly. But the fact that they come and hear me is very important, because they come despite that. And they want to discuss, and the main reason for that is because I have a Muslim name, and I come from the culture, so to that extent I say: "yeah, of course". Isaac Deutscher wrote a book called *The non-Jewish Jew*, which is what I feel we are within Muslim cultures. Those of us who have lived in that culture, grown up in it, appreciate it, without being religious. It is when I debate with young people that many things come to the fore, and one of the things is that the reason they say "we come and listen to you", is because they know I do not defend what the West is doing in Palestine and Iraq, and the people who do defend it. They name well-known Muslim writers or writers with Muslim names etc., "we will never trust them again. We don't believe a word they say, because they have been backing the West." So that's one of the problems, that there is a layer. We can name one name: Ayaan Hirsi Ali, it's filled with the most appalling rubbish, describing a tribal culture, from where she comes, and ascribing it to Islam. Because she is fashionable, it works. So this has spread around, and that drives people, kids especially, crazy. It is that sort of attitude which they hate, and when I discuss it with them they're quite open. Often they say to me: "we wish you were a believer", and I say: "well you can carry on wishing, and I wish you were non-believers", but that's the sort of debate which is nice to have, and I have it.

Q. *You complain that you can't find any decent books coming out of American academia, because of Saudi money. Can you elaborate on that? And isn't it also happening in Britain? And in that case, is it not also happening in Europe? And what are the implications of this, I'd like to ask you this, since this is a university context.*

A. This was a throw-away line, because most of my academic friends are in the States, and not in Britain, so I know more about it. But it happens in Britain too that most of the Arab Studies departments are funded by them, and I'm sure the same applies to Europe. And of course you don't bite the hand that feeds you. It's not even that they would put a formal condition on it, but people know not to do so. Having said that, I've nearly finished reading, because I'm reviewing it, an absolutely wonderful book on Saudi Arabia by an American academic called Robert Vitalis. He teaches in the Bay Area and the title of the book is *America's Kingdom*, and it's one of the most interesting accounts of the origins of this kingdom, and the links between this kingdom and the Aramco Oil Company, and what each learned from the other. He has been researching it for 25 years, and now he has published it. So this is an exception to the rule, but then he is not working for any Arab Studies department. It's a wonderful book, but these are few. The lessons for scholarship are obvious. It's a form of financial censorship: "we pay you, so you can't write against us". It would be very sad if this became more widespread on campuses – academics should be free to research what they want, and this research should not be controlled by any state or agency.

And we know perfectly well that in countries like Pakistan or even Indonesia, it is virtually impossible to read a critique of Saudi Arabia in the press, however free the papers might be. This shows how nervous and insecure they are. The only time you saw a massive critique emerging was in the three or four weeks after 9/11, but then it ended again. About six weeks ago I was travelling in Europe, and I was at an airport, so I bought all the big papers, which I sometimes do to compare them. Interestingly enough, from the British press through the *Herald Tribune*, *El País*, *Le Monde* and the *Süddeutsche Zeitung*, to the *Frankfurter Allgemeine Zeitung*, they had one story, the same story appeared in all these papers: that was an account of how Saudi Arabia was now re-educating and retraining the terrorists, and it was based on five so-called terrorists who had decided to change their way of life after going to a special school set up by the Saudi state. It was obviously a PR story, and it was published in every single paper, without anyone saying that this was in fact supplied to them by the Saudi Ministry of Propaganda.

List of Contributors

Ludo A. Abicht (Ostend, Belgium, 1936), MA in Germanic Studies (Ghent) and PhD in German Studies (Cincinnati), is visiting professor of philosophy and ethics at the University of Ghent (Belgium) and part time professor of Middle Eastern Studies at the University of Antwerp. He held visiting professorships in i.a. New Brunswick (Fredericton, Canada), Antioch University, Yellow Springs, UC Berkeley. He received the 2001 'Freedom of Speech' award. He is a Member of the Royal Dutch Academy of Language and Literature. One of his leading publications in Belgium is the book entitled *De joden van België* [The Jews in Belgium] (Amsterdam, 1994). Ludo Abicht published more than 120 articles, essays and chapters in journals such as *New German Critique, Monthly Review, Athenäum, Streven, Civis Mundi, Tijdschrift voor Diplomatie, Kreatief, Ons Erfdeel, Etcetera, Kultuurleven, Nieuw Wereldtijdschrift, Mores, Leesidee*, etc.

Sadik al-Azm (1934) studied philosophy at the American University of Beirut (AUB) and obtained his MA and PhD in modern European philosophy from Yale University. He taught i.a. at Yale, Hunter college in New York, Damascus University, Princeton University, Humboldt University in Berlin and in many other places. From 1969 to 1976 he was the editor of the *Arab Studies Review*. During his forty years career in academia, Sadik al-Azm emphasized the history of Western philosophy and wrote extensively on contemporary Arab society, culture and thought. His most renowned works are *Critique of Religious Thought* (1969) which turned into one of the biggest literary scandals that the Arab world had seen until then, and *Salman Rushdie and the Truth of Literature* (2002) in which he takes the defence of the author of *The Satanic Verses*. He was awarded the Dr. Leopold Lucks Prize for 2004 by the Tübingen University; he shared the Erasmus Prize (Holland) for 2004, with Fatima Mernissi and Abdul Karim Soroush. He is Doctor Honoris Causa (2005) of the University of Hamburg.

Tariq Ali (Lahore, Pakistan, 1943) is an author, filmmaker and historian. He is a prolific creative writer, he has written over a dozen books on world history and politics, several novels and scripts for both stage and screen. He was educated at Oxford University. Tariq Ali is perhaps best known for his work as a long-time member of the editorial committee of *New Left Review* and his non-fictional works of political biography, history and politics. His political writings centre on the divisions and tensions between East and West, between the Christian West and the world of Islam. He regularly contributes to *The Guardian, Counterpunch* and *the London Review of Books*. He is a regular broadcaster on BBC Radio. His fiction includes a series of historical novels about Islam: *Shadows of the Pomegranate Tree* (1992), *The Book of Saladin* (1998), *The Stone Woman* (2000) and *A Sultan in Palermo* (2005). His non-fiction includes 1968: *Marching in the Streets* (1998), a social history of the 1960s. His important book of essays, *The Clash of Fundamentalisms*, was published in 2002: in this book he puts the events of the September 11 attacks in historical perspective, covering the history of Islam from its foundations until today. Tariq Ali is a figurehead for critics of American foreign policy across the world.

John R. Bowen is the Dunbar-Van Cleve Professor in Arts & Sciences at Washington University in St. Louis. His long-term fieldwork has been in Indonesia, particularly in Aceh, and is most recently reflected in his book *Islam, Law and Equality in Indonesia: An Anthropology of Public Reasoning* (Cambridge, 2003). Current research on Islam and the state in France is reflected in *Why the French Don't Like Headscarves* (Princeton, 2007), and his next book, *Can Islam be French?* will appear from Princeton in 2008, followed by *The New Anthropology of Islam* from Cambridge.

Roger Dillemans was born in Belgium in 1932. He is married and they have four sons. He studied law and philosophy at the Catholic University of Leuven. He studied at Harvard University (LLM 1958) and at the Sorbonne (C.N.R.S.). He started an academic career at the Law Faculty in Leuven in 1960. He was dean of the Faculty. He was rector and president of the Board of Leuven University from 1985 to 1995. For some time he was chairman of the Flemish Science Policy Council, of the Confederation of Social Profit Enterprises, and of the Council of Culture in Flanders. He was cofounder and president of the European Institute of Social Security, visiting professor King's College, London, former advisor in the Cabinet of the Prime Minister and president of Caritas Catholica. He is member of the Board of Leuven University and of the Association K.U.Leuven, member of the Liaison Agency Flanders-Europe, honorary member of the Brussels Bar, honorary Royal Commissioner for the Restatement of the Belgian Social Security System. Doctor Honoris Causa of seven universities.

List of Contributors

Mark Eyskens, Minister of state, occupied important ministerial functions (1976-92) i.a. as prime minister and minister of foreign affairs and finance of Belgium. He is doctor in law and economics, bac. philisophy (K.U.Leuven) and M.A. economics (Columbia University, New York). He is professor em. economics at the Catholic University of Leuven and former member of the Belgian Parliament (1977-2003), of the Council of Europe and the Assembly of the WEU (1993-2003). He is past president of the Royal Flemish Academy of Belgium for Sciences and Arts and president of the Francqui Foundation and other scientific and cultural institutions. He is member of the board of the International Crisis Group and of the board of several Belgian and foreign companies. He is the author of thirty eight books (three novels) and numerous articles and also a Sunday afternoon painter. He was awarded several prizes (Prize Scriptores Christiani; Benelux-Europa Prize; Plaquette d'or de l'Académie des Sciences, Arts et Lettres de France …)

Marie-Claire Foblets, Lic. Iur., Lic. Phil., Ph. D. Anthrop. (Leuven, Belgium). Professor ordinarius of Law and Anthropology at the Universities of Leuven, Brussels and Antwerp. She held various visiting professorships, i.a. at Paris/Sorbonne. In 2001 she was elected Member of the Royal Academy of Sciences and Arts ('Vlaamse Koninklijke Academie voor Wetenschappen'). She is a honorary member of the Brussels bar. In 2004 she received the Francqui Prize. She has done extensive research and published widely on issues of immigration, integration and nationality law in Belgium. In the field of anthropology of law, her research focuses on the application of Islamic family laws in Europe.

Tariq Modood is Professor of Sociology, Politics and Public Policy and the founding Director of the Centre for the Study of Ethnicity and Citizenship at the University of Bristol. He has published over 30 (co-)authored and (co-) edited books and reports and over ninety articles or chapters in political philosophy, sociology and public policy and co-founded the international journal, *Ethnicities*. He is a regular contributor to the media and policy debates in Britain was awarded a MBE for services to social sciences and ethnic relations in 2001 and elected a member of the Academy of Social Sciences in 2004. His recent publications include *Multicultural Politics: Racism, Ethnicity and Muslims in Britain* (Edinburgh and Minnesota University Presses, 2005), *Multiculturalism: A Civic Idea* (Polity Press, 2007); and as co-editor, *Multiculturalism, Muslims and Citizenship: A European Approach* (Routledge, 2006).

Rudolph (Ruud) Peters (1943) teaches Arabic and Islamic studies at the University of Amsterdam. From 1982-1987 he was director of the Netherlands-Flemish Institute in Cairo. His research focuses on *jihad* (*Jihad in Classical and Modern Islam* (2nd rev. ed.), Princeton, Wiener, 2005), on Islamic criminal law (*Crime and Punishment in Islamic Law*, Cambridge, Cambridge University Press, 2005; *Islamic Criminal Law in Nigeria*, Ibadan, Spectrum, 2003; many articles on Islamic criminal law in 19th century Egypt) and on Islam in Europe. He has been an expert witness in several trials of persons suspected of Islamist extremism.

Jean Pierre Rondas was editor in chief and is now a senior producer of the cultural talk programmes of Klara, the 'Classical Radio' of VRT (Vlaamse Radio en Televisie, the Dutch speaking Public Broadcast Service in Belgium). He was born in Ghent in 1946 and studied comparative literature and philosophy at the University of Ghent. He wrote a study on J.R.R. Tolkien's mythopoeic romances, translated the part on *The Beautiful* of Immanuel Kant's *Kritik der Urteilskraft* into Dutch, made radio serials on Joyce's *Ulysses* and *Finnegans Wake*, and wrote several essays on Umberto Eco's semiotic novels. During 15 years he ran the only radio magazine in the Low Countries devoted exclusively to German culture and society. He runs his own weekly Sunday morning interview programme 'Rondas' (formerly better called 'Worldviews'), with interviews in Dutch, English, French and German, in the spheres of the humanities and the social sciences. Last year, he published his *Rondas' Wereldbeeldenboek* [Rondas' Book of Worldviews] with interviews with contemporary philosophers.

Bassam Tibi (Damascus, Syria, 1944) is Professor of International Relations in Goettingen (Germany). He has earned his research reputation through his books worldwide. He held various visiting scholarships, i.a. at Harvard, Princeton, Berkeley and Ann Arbor, in Turkey, Sudan, Cameroun, Indonesia and Singapore. Since 2004 he holds the A.D. White Professorship-at-large, Cornell University, USA. He is also a member of the Fundamentalism project of the American Academy of Arts and Sciences. Bassam Tibi has published numerous books, in English and in German (translated in 16 languages), i.a. *The Challenge of Fundamentalism* (California U.P., 2002); *Islam Between Culture and Politics* (Palgrave, expanded new edition 2005). His publications deal with Islamic civilization, the Middle East and the Mediterranean region. Additionally, he has published in leading journals such as *International Journal of Middle Eastern Studies, Millenium, The Fletcher Forum, Human Rights Quarterly, Middle East Journal* and in encyclopedias such as *The Oxford Encyclopedia of Modern Islam, Routledge Encyclopedia of Government and Politics* and *Encyclopedia of Democracy.* He is board member of several significant institutions and the recipient of many prizes. In 1995 he was awarded the Medal of the (German) State; in 2003 he received the annual prize of the Swiss Foundation for European Awareness.

Nasr H. Abu Zayd (Egypt, 1943), MA in Arabic and Islamic Studies (Faculty of Arts, Cairo University); Ph.D. in Arabic and Islamic Studies (Faculty of Arts, Cairo University), holds the Ibn Rushd Chair at the University of Humanistics, Utrecht (the Netherlands). He is also professor of Islamic Studies at the University of Leiden (the Netherlands). He is former Professor of Arabic literature at Cairo University. For his persistent battle for independent scientific research of the *Qur'ân*, he has received the The 1998 Jordanian Writers Association Award for Democracy and Freedom, the 2005 Ibn Rushd Prize for Freedom of Thought and in the 2006 Prize of freedom of thought by the Muslim Democrats Society in Denmark. Nasr Abu Zayd has published fourteen Arabic Books – most of them have enjoyed translation to most of the Muslim's languages, such as Turkish, Indonesian and Farsi as well as translation to European languages – in addition to countless published papers in Arabic and English. The following titles are just examples: *Politik und Islam: Kritik des Religiösen Diskurses*, translated by Cherifa Magdi, Dipa-Verlag, Frankfurt, 1996; *Ein Leben mit dem Islam* [Life with Islam] autobiography edited by Navid Kirmani, translated by Sharifa Magdi, Herder, 1999; *Critique du Discours Religieux*, translated by M. Chairet, Sindbad Actes Sud, 1999; *Voice of an Exile* (coauthor: Esther R. Nelson), Praeger, Greenwood Publishing Group, USA, 2004; *Rethinking the Qur'ân: Towards a Humanistic Hermeneutics*, The Humanistic University Press Publication, 2004; *Reformation of Islamic Thought: A Critical Historical Analysis*, WRR-Verkenning no 10, Amsterdam University Press, 2006.

www.ingramcontent.com/pod-product-compliance
Ingram Content Group UK Ltd.
Pitfield, Milton Keynes, MK11 3LW, UK
UKHW041914140426
5217IPUK00013B/152